Letting Go for Love

Kris Francoeur

Letting Go for Love is a work of fiction. Names, characters, places, and incidents are the product of the author's imagination or are used fictitiously. Any resemblance to actual events, locales, or persons, living or dead, is coincidental.

Willow River Press is an imprint of Between the Lines Publishing. The Willow River Press name and logo are trademarks of Between the Lines Publishing.

Copyright © 2021 by Kris Francoeur

Cover design by Cherie Fox

Between the Lines Publishing and its imprints supports the right to free expression and the value of copyright. The scanning, uploading, and distribution of this book without permission is a theft of the author's intellectual property. If you would like permission to use material from the book (other than for review purposes), please contact info@btwnthelines.com.

> Between the Lines Publishing
> 9 North River Road, Ste 248
> Auburn ME 04210
> btwnthelines.com

First Published: November 2021

ISBN: (Paperback) 978-1-950502-55-4

ISBN: (Ebook) 978-1-950502-56-1

Library of Congress Control Number: 2021948775

The publisher is not responsible for websites (or their content) that are not owned by the publisher.

Letting Go for Love

Kris Francoeur

For Sebastian, who I wish I had met, and for his mom, Jami.

As always, for Sam, who believed.

Prologue

Dot sat on the edge of her bed, her feet dangling above the cold floor of her room. Was she really getting up this early on Thanksgiving? God, a day to sleep in as long as she wanted seemed like a fantasy. She was so tired.

Shaking her head, she sighed. "Suck it up, buttercup. This is life. Be thankful you only have to make a pie for today."

With that, she placed her feet on the ice-cold floor, shivered, and headed to the shower.

Afterwards, Dot poured a cup of coffee, sneaking a glance at the clock on the wall. She had twenty minutes before she needed to wake the boys, so, if she focused, she could get the next section of the application done.

She opened her laptop and clicked on the tab. Seeing the form populate with the work she had already done, she paused. Was it worth even trying? Yes, it was. She needed this grant. She had already made it through the first round of the application process; this was a much more comprehensive version.

She leaned back in her chair, daydreaming for just a moment. If she was awarded the money, she would be able to paint full-time for a whole year; the foundation would pay her enough to cover her bills. And she could *paint*. She could take advantage of natural daylight instead of limiting herself to those late-night hours when the boys slept. It would be a dream come true.

It was a long shot, but she had to try.

Chapter One

It had been an odd couple of days. Really odd. Just as he had done many times before, Boone had traveled to Vermont several days ago with his best friend PJ to spend Thanksgiving. As before, they were going to celebrate with PJ's twin sister Georgiana. Georgie. Gigi. The pain-in-the-ass at times.

Boone smiled to himself. Georgie (or Gigi, depending on his mood and the situation) was a force in his life, and had been for a long time. For years, they had been dearest friends, and even lovers at one point, although they had never fallen in love with each other. Now she was with Jack, and her happiness and sense of peace warmed Boone's heart, while also making him feel slightly alone in the world.

Georgiana and Jack were so happy together, it was wonderful. Really, it was. Yes, Boone had been with Georgiana for a long time, but more in a friends-with-benefits kind of way. It was great to see her so content, but now he was feeling a bit out of his element. He had stayed with Georgiana for years, upon each visit to Vermont. At first, he stayed there as friends, then lovers, then as best friends. Now that she was engaged to another man, it no longer felt right, so he was now staying in a small apartment connected to the farm's big barn.

Boone shook his head. Enough with the self-pity and thoughts of loneliness. His best friends were happy as hell, and he was lucky to have them in his life. He decided a run might work the foul mood out of his system. A brisk ten miles would do his spirit a world of good and justify the multiple pieces of pie he planned to eat at the holiday dinner.

Later, Boone stood in the middle of the road. Shock coursed through him. He tried to slow his breathing as the snowflakes landed on his face. The cold of the snow helped focus his mind on what he had just heard. "You are kidding me, right? All three of you?"

Jack was the first to nod, his smile spreading across his entire face. "All three of us. Not planned, shocked the hell outta all of us, but yes."

Boone still needed to understand. "All three of you got engaged last night. Are you fucking kidding me? I leave you alone for one goddamn night, trying to let you have time to have the whole family dinner thing with Jack's family, and all three of you get engaged?"

Shroom laughed. "In all fairness, I proposed to Mark on Sunday night, but after Jack and Georgie made their announcement last night, we hopped on the wagon too."

PJ put his arm around Boone. "And you know that I've been planning on proposing to Julia. I thought I'd do it on Thanksgiving, but after Mom announced she's finally getting married, I couldn't stand waiting anymore, and I proposed last night." He shook his head at Jack. "Imagine my surprise when we came back over here last night to announce our news, and the damn house was rocking with *everyone* celebrating engagements!"

Boone's voice cracked as he gave PJ a boisterous squeeze and a hearty slap on the back. "Congrats, man. Jules is awesome; I'm happy for you both." He turned to Shroom. "And Shroom, that is so amazing," he said, hugging his friend. Finally, he turned toward Jack. "Shit, Jack. I am so amazed, and this is so very cool."

Jack stepped forward and hugged Boone hard. "Thanks, Boone." he said.

Boone continued to shake his head. "Damn. Wow."

PJ laughed. "Now we just need to find you a good woman."

"Or man," said Shroom. "Remember, we're open minded around here."

Chapter Two

A half hour later, Boone flopped onto the bed in the small apartment. He knew he needed to start house-hunting to prepare for his permanent move to Vermont in March, but for now he enjoyed the bit of privacy the apartment provided.

Lying on the bed, he watched the morning light play across the ceiling. He thought back to the morning's conversation and shook his head again. PJ, Jack, and Shroom all engaged within days of each other. Georgiana was engaged. For a moment, he felt lonely again, realizing that his life was transforming at what felt like the speed of light.

His phone buzzed on the table next to the bed. Looking at the screen, he smiled, seeing a text from Georgiana. *Hey, you around? If so, come have breakfast with us.*

He typed back. *You mean you need help setting up and figure you can bribe me with blueberry muffins?*

Yeah, yeah. No, I have plenty of help over here, but we'd love to see you.

Did he want to go over or not? He did. *Be there in ten.*

Stepping onto the front porch, Boone reached for the doorknob, then stopped. He had walked right into this house for so many years. But Georgiana and Jack were now living together and planning to marry. Was it presumptuous to still walk in?

The door opened, and Georgiana peered at him through the screen. "What the hell are you doing?"

"Trying to figure out if I should knock. I mean, I've always just walked in, but now…"

She pushed the screen door open. "Get in here."

Georgiana hugged him. "I still love you, Boonie. Always will. As for future visits, if we know you're coming, just walk in. Otherwise, knock."

"Fair enough."

In the kitchen, Georgiana poured Boone a cup of coffee and handed it to him. He smiled and pulled a basket of muffins toward him, putting one on the small white plate in front of him. "What time did Grandma Ruth get up to make these?"

"I don't know, I slept later than usual. Probably around six. She made them, cleaned up the kitchen, then took a walk to PJ's with another basket of them." She sipped her coffee and looked at him over the rim. "You okay with all this?"

"What do you mean?"

"I mean, you're already retiring from the military and moving, and now the rest of us are getting married. Change is in the air."

He saw the concern on Georgiana's face. Other than PJ, she was his closest friend in the world. He took another sip as he chose his words. "It doesn't really matter whether I'm okay with it, Gigi. It is what it is."

Her expression reflected immediate concern, and a flash of hurt. "Boone…"

He shrugged. "No, seriously, Gi. It is. I'm not trying to whine or be a shit."

She tried to smile. "Really?"

He laughed. "I'm just calling it like I see it. Shroom marrying Mark? That's awesome. And I knew PJ would propose eventually." He reached over and squeezed her hand. "And as for you, I am so happy for you. And I mean that. I can't imagine anyone better for you than Jack. I have never seen you this happy and at peace, never. So, yes, I'm good with it all."

Jack walked into the kitchen and chuckled as he moved to stand behind Georgiana. "Good thing I heard a lot of that as I came down the stairs, otherwise I might be concerned to see the two of you holding hands."

Georgiana tipped her head back and he leaned down to kiss her. "Yeah, yeah," she teased. "I think your position here is pretty secure."

Jack playfully ruffled his fiancée's hair then poured himself a cup of coffee. He snagged a muffin as he sat. "I think so, too," he said. He stroked her left hand, resting a finger over her engagement ring. "Especially now."

Chapter Three

Dot sighed as she pulled into the parking lot of the hockey rink. How could coaches expect kids to practice on a holiday? Despite today being voluntary, every hockey parent knew that if their kid missed it, he warmed the bench for the next few games. Dot knew this very idea could set her oldest off, so here she was, on Thanksgiving morning, with two boys and their hockey equipment in tow.

She looked over her shoulder at her youngest son, Finn, and tried to sound calm. "I know you don't want to sit through Dec's practice after yours, but I need to run errands. He's going to watch yours, so you watch his. I'll be back to get you, we'll run home, get cleaned up, then go to George's for Thanksgiving, got it?"

Finn rolled his eyes. "Why do I have to wait here? Why can't I just leave my gear in the locker room and walk around town with the guys?"

"Because ten-year-olds don't walk around town without supervision. Declan has his phone and can call if you guys need me. I'm going to get everything done quickly, and if there's time, I'll be back to watch." She smiled pleadingly. "Please, buddy. Just don't make it an issue. I really need to get the door fixed."

Finn's determination to assert his independence warred with his well-honed desire to not upset his mom. His tone was sullen but resigned. "Fine," he said.

After getting both boys to the locker room with their overstuffed hockey bags, and double-checking that the coach had her number, Dot returned to her car. How she wished she could just go home, make cocoa, and lie on the couch with an episode of *Outlander* without worrying about the boys walking in on a sex scene. That was not an option today. Shit, when was that *ever* an option? She was the single parent of two busy boys, juggling her house, family, and career.

Despite today being a holiday, Dot had chores that needed to be done on this rare day off from work. She needed to gas up the car, run to Home Depot for the materials to fix the lock on the front door, then go home and fix it, make a pie, and return to the rink to collect the boys. If she hurried, maybe she could get a Dunkaccino between stops. For a moment, she felt a tiny swell of frustration, almost a "poor me" moment, as she realized how much she would like a day away from being an adult. A day with a pedicure, meals she didn't have to cook or clean up after, and a day with which she could do exactly as she wanted.

Enough self-pity, she thought. She had married a great man and had two great kids. Yes, her husband's death had left her widowed when the boys were very young, but she had made a nice life for the three of them. She loved her job, had good friends, had a great dog, and loved their little community. There were many not half as lucky as she was. Still, an hour on the couch looking at the fine Scotsman would be a hell of a delightful treat.

Standing outside her car as she filled the tank, Dot stomped her feet on the snowy wet pavement, mentally kicking herself for not wearing boots today. What self-respecting Vermonter wore sneakers in November?

She tucked her hands deep into the pockets of her down jacket, bouncing in place to keep warm. A deep male voice cut through the air. "Dot?"

Peering around the back of her car, Dot felt the shock ripple through her as she realized it was Boone, Georgiana's Boone, who was standing on the other side of the gas pump. She acknowledged the incredible rush of physical attraction but was simultaneously aware of the searing embarrassment over her appearance. Ratty jeans, frumpy jacket, winter hat, and, of all things, sneakers. "Boone!" she exclaimed.

He walked around her car, smiling from ear to ear. "Hey, it's so good to see you." He opened his arms. "I feel like it's been forever."

"Me too," she said. "You here for Thanksgiving?" Dot moved into his hug, willing herself to set aside how good he smelled, or how nicely those jeans fit him. Jesus, she was more desperate for a man than she thought.

"Oh course," he enthused. "We came up early and we'll head back on Saturday."

The pump clicked, and before Dot could move, Boone said, "I got that." He placed the nozzle back on the pump, put the gas cap on, then closed the hatch. "You're coming to holiday dinner, right?"

"I am," she said. "I need to run some errands and get stuff done at home, but then we'll be over."

"Need help?"

Dot tried to mask her shock, unsure she had heard him correctly. "Huh?"

Boone leaned against her car, clearly comfortable in the conversation and oblivious to how she was giving him the once-over. "Gigi has everything organized, and with Jack there too, I felt like a bit of a third wheel, so I'm killing some time. If there's anything I can do to help, it would keep me busy."

"Well, I'm headed over to Home Depot to get a new lockset for my front door, then I need to go install it. The door isn't locking any more, and… well, even though it's pretty safe around here, I don't like the house being open all the time. Y-you're welcome to keep me company," she stammered.

He looked at her curiously, and Dot tried to not stare into his chocolate brown eyes and study their impossibly long lashes. "Do you know how to install a lockset?"

She looked down at her feet. "No. But I mean, I can read, and follow a YouTube video. I'm pretty handy, I can figure it out."

He chuckled as he stepped around her to open the car door. "Here, get in. I'll follow you to Home Depot, you can get what you need, then I'll help you install it. I've changed countless locks over the years."

Dot felt like a teenager again, awkward, and gawky, trying to sound intelligent as she slid into the driver's seat. "You don't have to. I can do it, Boone, really."

"I'm sure you can." He stood with his hand on her doorframe. "But come on, Dot, help me out here. Otherwise, I'm truly going to drive around town looking for something to do to burn the next couple hours, or I'll end up going back to the farm and sitting in the apartment until everyone arrives. Either way, I'll feel like a jerk. At least if I help you with the lock, it's like I had a plan for the day."

How could she say no? "Fine," she laughed, "see you at Home Depot."

Thirty minutes later, Dot pulled into her driveway with Boone driving in right behind her. She got out of the car and pulled a bag from the front seat. Suddenly, he was next to her. "Here, give me that, and point me toward any tools you have."

Opening the back door, Dot was pleased with herself for taking a few extra minutes to pick up before leaving the house that morning. Having Boone walk into the routine chaos would have been an enormous embarrassment. "Come on in." She gestured toward the kitchen. "Would you like coffee or something? Tea? Hot chocolate?"

Boone's eyebrows shot up hopefully. "Hot chocolate?"

Dot stifled a laugh. "Really? I was standing at the gas station thinking all I wanted to do was come home and have cocoa…"

"That's awesome. PJ gives me shit because I'd rather drink cocoa than coffee most of the time."

"Me too. One cup of coffee in the morning, one more if George is on the warpath at work, but that's it."

"Yeah, when she's on the warpath we all need extra caffeine. That's how I do it, too. I had my usual cup of joe with one of Ruth's muffins this morning."

"Her blueberry ones?" Her tone reflected her love for those muffins.

"Yup." He laughed. "I think it's funny how we all love them, and she knows it. She won't tell anyone, not even Georgie, how she makes the damn things. No one makes them like she does. Anyway, more than two coffees a day and I'm climbing the walls. But I admit I'm a sucker for a good hot chocolate." He shrugged. "So, tell me, how's she been at work lately?"

Dot had been Georgiana's assistant since she'd become the principal at the local school, and over the years, they had developed a deep friendship as well. "She's been good. Still tires easily, but now that she can be there almost full-time again, she feels back in control." She chuckled. "You know Georgie, those days of having to rest made her insane. She was sure that everything was falling apart at school because she wasn't there running the ship."

"Yeah, she does have control issues." Boone shook his head, "But now, with Jack, she seems to have found some sort of peace."

"I know. She's happy."

"She is." Boone nodded. "She is, and I'm glad."

"Me too," she said. "Time for work. I'll make us some hot chocolate, then you can teach me all you know about locksets."

An hour later, Boone stood at Dot's kitchen sink, washing his hands. He called back over his shoulder, "Do the mugs go in the dishwasher?"

Dot was in the pantry, pulling the pie ingredients from the shelves. She stopped for a moment, still trying to wrap her brain around the fact that this gorgeous man had just helped her install the new lock. "Yeah. Don't worry about rinsing them."

As she came back into the kitchen, balancing the items in her arms, he practically jumped across the room. "Here, give me those before you drop them."

She tried not to notice his hand brushing hers as she relinquished the chocolate and maple syrup. "Thanks," she said.

"So, what are you making?"

Dot set the oven to preheat. "Pecan pie."

His tone was one of disbelief as he scanned the ingredients. "You're the one who makes the chocolate maple pecan pie?"

She nodded. "That's me."

"That is my absolute favorite dessert at George's Thanksgiving." He looked embarrassed. "Shit, Dot, I always cut a slice before dinner and hide it on top of the fridge, so I don't miss out."

"You do?"

"I do."

"Wow." What the heck was she supposed to do with him now, still standing in her kitchen? "Want to help?"

"Sure," he said.

Dot motioned to the cupboards on the far wall. "There's a dark blue bowl on the top shelf. If you can get it down, I'll get the eggs and butter."

Boone turned around just seconds later, and before he could stop himself, he was awash with hormones as he watched her bend over. Damn, she was a fine-looking woman. No, not just fine-looking.

She was spectacular. Just his type. He loved how she was petite but curvy, and strong. He could see sleek arm muscles flexing as she worked, and it was hot. The funny thing was, she did not even realize it. He let himself gawk for a moment, secure in the fact she could not see him. Her curves were everything any red-blooded man would want in a woman.

As Dot stood up and turned, Boone quickly averted his eyes. Dot strode over to the table, dumping the rest of the ingredients next to the blue bowl. "Are your hands clean?"

He laughed. "You sound like my mom," he said. "Yes, they're clean."

"If you already washed them, then your mom did a good job," she mused. She went on to recite her recipe from memory. "Crack four eggs into the bowl and mix in a cup of maple syrup."

As Boone followed her instructions, Dot rolled a crust over the pie plate, then pressed it into place, crimping the edges just so. When Boone was done mixing the filling, she poured it into the plate, then carefully placed it on a foil-lined pan and slid it into the hot oven.

After setting the timer, she turned back to Boone. "Done. Now it bakes for an hour, we put it on the porch to cool, then look forward to eating it."

Chapter Four

Boone looked at his watch as he finished drying the few dishes that they couldn't squeeze into the dishwasher. "Unless you need help with something else, I guess I should head back to the farm."

"Thanks, Boone, I'm all set." Dot tucked a strand of her auburn hair behind her ear. "I'm going to set up the easel for tonight, get cleaned up, then get the boys from the rink."

Boone was headed toward his coat but he stopped. "The easel?"

"Yeah. I finished stretching a new canvas last night. I figured I can paint for a while when the boys are in a food coma later."

He looked confused. "You paint?" Suddenly, Boone's gaze locked on something behind her, and Dot turned to see what had caught his interest. "That's like the paintings in Georgie's house." Dot waited for him to put the pieces together. "Wait, did you paint those?"

She nodded, unsure what to say.

His eyes widened. "I have always loved those paintings." He leaned against the doorframe. "Shit, Dot... I guess I always assumed she had picked them up in her travels or something." He smiled and looked directly at her. "You are incredibly talented."

Dot fought the urge to squirm like a puppy under his praise. "Thanks, it's just a hobby."

Boone picked his words carefully. "Look, not that it's my business, but it should be more than a hobby. You are really good. Why don't you try to go pro with it?"

Should she tell him about the grant application? Hell, no. No one, not even Georgiana or her boys knew about it. "I'd love to someday, but until then, bills need to be paid, so I need the steady paycheck. But when I can take the time to paint, I do. That's why I want to set up the easel before I get the boys."

"Then I'll get out of your hair, and I'll see you at the farm," he said with a wink.

Back at the farm, Boone walked into the apartment and hung his coat on the peg by the door. For the first time in years, he felt completely free to date someone, and then suddenly, he had spent the afternoon with Dot.

Ever since he and Georgiana had first become lovers, he had felt the need to avoid getting involved with anyone else. Even after they agreed to no longer be physically intimate, he remained uncomfortable with the idea of dating anyone. But now Georgiana was head over heels in love with a great guy, and if he was honest with himself, he had to admit he had always found Dot attractive. It wasn't like she had ever tried to get his attention. Shit, in fact, she had done the opposite. He knew she'd been widowed years before, but it was like she had completely turned off the woman side of herself.

He thought about her as he poured a glass of water. Cold water. Frankly, he'd rather pour himself a stiff drink, but it was still early in the day for that.

Dot… That bright auburn hair, worn in a simple bob, sometimes pulled back in a barrette. Those hazel eyes, the sprinkling of freckles on her nose. Damn, she was attractive as hell, and the fact that she seemed unaware of it made her even more desirable. He knew she had curves that could drive a man insane under those simple clothes she usually wore. Seeing her in jeans and that winter hat today made him want to grab her by the hand and run off to find a campfire where he could sit and hear her entire life story.

With a shake of his head, Boone looked up at the ceiling. Time to cool off and get ready for Thanksgiving dinner. Nothing was going to happen between them now, but maybe when he moved to Vermont?

Chapter Five

It was mid-afternoon when guests began arriving, parking along both sides of the road, by the barn, in front of the garage, and wedging their cars into any other space they could find. Jack stood in the barn door with Boone, having just walked over to find him at the apartment. "Good lord! When Charlie said the entire town was coming, I didn't think he meant it literally."

Boone laughed. "Welcome to the mayhem, Jack. This is how Gigi does stuff. She was lonely when she took over the house. That first year, she opened Thanksgiving up to anyone who had nowhere else to go, and it's just grown from there." He waved a hand toward the cars. "This is just the beginning; I can assure you."

An hour later, Boone stood next to Jack and Georgiana, holding a beer in his hand. As the crowd chatted, Georgiana's grandfather James raised his glass and clinked it with a spoon. "Hey, all of you, quiet down."

The crowd went silent, and Jack realized that most of the guests knew the rituals of this gathering. He smiled as he looked across the room, where his parents stood with Georgiana's mom and dad. It still shocked him to think that his fiancée had just met her father for the first time just days before. The way she had come through so much and stayed so sane and positive amazed him.

James adjusted his glasses as he referred to a piece of paper extracted from the pocket of his sportscoat. "First, let's take a moment to remember and celebrate those we lost in the past year." He looked around the room until his eyes settled on an elderly woman seated on the couch. "Ginny, we honor Pete, and we miss him." His eyes moved to look at another elderly woman. "And we miss Patrick." He turned his attention to a mournful younger woman. "And Tina, we miss Brad more than we can say." He raised his glass. "To those we have lost."

"To those we have lost," the room chorused.

James smiled. "Now it's time for our more joyous celebrations." Over the next five minutes, he spoke of the happier moments the group had experienced – the births, the college acceptances, and the marriages, with each announcement met by plenty of enthusiastic clapping and cheering. "Okay," James said, "I have a bunch of Hewitt celebrations to announce, and since I have the floor, you all have to shut up and listen."

He looked lovingly across the room toward Shroom. "Our son Jason brought the most amazing man into our lives, Michael, who most of you," he chuckled, "refer to as Shroom. We love him like blood, and we already consider him a son. With that said, it is my absolute pleasure to announce that Michael and Mark will be getting married next month. Mark, welcome to the family!"

When the applause died down, James looked at his daughter, smiling. "And just this week we have had the absolute pleasure of getting to know George Payton James, Gia and PJ's father; George and Kathryn are also now engaged." More applause rang through the room.

James laughed and gestured for the crowd to quiet. "I also have the pleasure of announcing that PJ and Boone will make their permanent move to Vermont in March, as PJ and Julia are also officially engaged to be married."

Dot stood in the kitchen doorway and tried to assimilate the news. Who was she kidding? Assimilate it? She had almost dropped her wine glass. Boone was moving to Vermont. Permanently. Not just for a quick visit before returning to base. How was she ever going to keep from doing something stupid around him? She tried to keep the apparent shock off her face by talking herself into a pleased but neutral look. Shit, if she had known, she wouldn't have had him over this morning. It was one thing to be a bit flirty when she thought he would be headed back to Virginia at the end of the weekend, not to be seen again for months, and completely another to know he was moving here soon. Shit, she had played with fire within herself without even knowing it.

Just then, Dot realized the crowd was laughing as they witnessed the joy emanating from James. "And yes, one more announcement," he said. "If that all wasn't enough, it is also my absolute pleasure to announce that Georgiana and Jack have decided to tie the knot."

Chapter Six

Three hours later, after eating an obscene amount of food, Dot tiredly rubbed her eyes as she tried to locate her pie plate in the kitchen.

Boone came in, hoping to find her, and fought the reaction he had felt when he first saw her in that dark green sweater dress and those black leather boots – much more dressed up than usual. Each year, he saw her at least a half-dozen times, and usually, she was in jeans and a t-shirt or a simple sweater. Even dressed her normal way, she was a beautiful woman, and she always got his attention, but in that outfit, she was making it hard for him to think clearly. Trying to be nonchalant, he smiled. "Hey, Dot, getting ready to head home?"

"Yeah." She walked over to look in the sink. "I can't find my pie plate."

He shrugged. "I will find it for you. It was the dark blue pottery one, right? With the white specks?"

"It is."

He motioned around, the kitchen full of dishes, all clean, but in piles. "Once the place clears out, I'm sure it will appear. I'll let you know when I find it." He pulled his phone from his pocket. "What's your number? I can text you."

Dot dutifully recited her number. She heard the soft tone as he saved her in his contacts. He smiled. "Done."

"Thanks, that would be great." Dot looked at him, her face troubled. "Why didn't you mention you were moving here when you were at my house today?" she blurted.

He thought for a moment, wondering if her question was an idle one, or if she actually cared that he would be around more. "I don't know. I guess I was probably still in shock from the whole everyone-is-getting-married conversation this morning, and we were having fun together, so I didn't think much about it." He suddenly looked unsure. "You had fun, didn't you?"

Dot felt herself melting. This beautiful man towered over her but was looking at her so sweetly, his dark eyes so sincere. "Yes, Boone, I had fun this morning. It was good to just hang out."

"I'm glad." He morphed back into the self-assured warrior she was more familiar with. "You let me know when you have anything else that needs to be fixed. All I charge is a hot cocoa."

"Deal," she laughed.

The next morning, Boone pulled his hoodie over his t-shirt, then shrugged into his down vest. Why the heck was it so cold this early? It was already feeling like a real Vermont winter. In just a few short months he would be living here full-time. He made a mental note to start buying a winter wardrobe now that he would be a civilian.

He pulled his phone from his pocket and texted, *Morning, Dot, it's Boone. I have your plate. I'm headed out to help Jack move and thought I could drop it off on my way. If you aren't home, I'll leave it by that securely locked door.*

Dot was standing in her kitchen when Boone's message came through, and she chuckled. Then her eyes widened. He was stopping by? Shit, she hadn't even brushed her teeth yet, having staggered out of bed to get the boys to practice, then home to have coffee and a breakfast of her own.

That would be awesome, thanks. If you tell me when, I'll have a to-go cup of cocoa for you.

Dot realized she was standing there, grinning like an idiot. Enough, she told herself. He was a friend. Hell, he was barely a friend, more like a long-term acquaintance. And until a year ago, he had frequented the bed of her closest female friend. And besides, she told herself, even if he was interested, which he probably wasn't, she didn't date. The boys needed a full-time, full-attention, no-distractions parent. She was the only one they had, and they needed all of her.

Looking at her watch, she sprinted up the stairs to brush her teeth, deciding along the way that a little eyeliner and mascara wouldn't hurt.

At exactly 9:30, Dot heard a car in her driveway. Shaking her head, she muttered, "Knock it off. He's just being nice, bringing the plate back, nothing more."

She opened the door just as he raised his hand to knock. "Hey," she said, smiling.

"Good morning." He held out the plate. "As promised."

"Thank you." She felt silly. "Come on in, I believe I promised you cocoa in exchange."

He smiled, causing that dimple to appear again. She felt her pulse race. He shrugged. "I'd never turn that down, but if you're busy…"

"Well, come on then."

In the kitchen, Dot quickly poured milk into the pan. "Can you stay and drink it, or do you need to get to Jack's right away?"

Even to his own ears, he sounded like he answered too quickly. "I can stay."

"Good, then have a seat."

Five minutes later, Dot put a mug in front of him and placed a cookie jar in the middle of the table. "Not Ruth's muffins," she said, "but passable."

She fetched her own mug, then sat across from him. "Good morning."

"Good morning."

"How was it after I left last night?"

Boone laughed. "Fine. Good, really. It was amusing to see Jack tell Georgie she was doing too much. Boy, you should have seen her face when he assured her the rest of us were capable of cleaning up."

"I take it she didn't handle it well."

"You know her as well as anyone. How well does she ever take orders?"

"Good point." She took a sip. "And you were recruited to help Jack move today?"

"Yes, ma'am." He snagged a cookie and took a bite.

Dot felt she needed to say what was on her mind. "Are you really okay with all of this?"

"With what?" He looked at her pointedly.

She struggled to choose the right words. "With a woman you loved now marrying another man."

His gaze locked on her as he wondered why she was asking. "To be clear, I still love George. But I was never *in* love with her, never was going to be. So, I'm thrilled for her." He tipped his head. "And while I never liked her ex-husband, I liked Jack from the first time we met. I can't imagine anyone else better for her."

"Oh," Dot nodded. "I'm glad you feel that way. I would hate to see your friendship change after all this time."

Boone tipped his head, "So, did you have time to paint last night?"

A safe topic, at last. "I did."

"Could I see it?"

Dot was shocked. "Y-you want to see my painting?"

"I do."

"But you understand it's not done; I just started it."

"I know. Dot, if you don't want to show me, just say so."

"No, it's not that…" She pushed her chair back. "C'mon, you can bring your mug with you."

She started up the stairs as Boone hurried to keep up.

On the second floor, she motioned to the first open door. "The boys' bathroom," she said, then motioned to the next door. "Their room. Ignore the mess, please." She continued to the last door off the hallway. "This is my room, and where I paint."

Boone slowly entered the room. Dot swallowed, suddenly nervous. No male other than her sons had been in her bedroom since Mike died. Wait, the plumber had. Make that, no man she found *attractive* had been in her bedroom. "This is what I was working on last night." She sounded unsure of herself as she stepped aside.

Boone stepped forward to get a better look. The large easel was set up in front of the windows, lights aimed over the sizable canvas, with painting supplies organized neatly nearby. The work-in-progress was clearly depicting a Vermont winter night, the moonlight glinting off a stream and the surrounding snowy fields. It was already stunning. "Dot, this is fabulous."

"Really? You like it?"

"I love it." He turned to look at her. "From memory, from a picture, or made up?"

She smiled. "A memory," she said. "Just a scene I came across on a run last winter. It was so beautiful, I guess it just stayed with me."

"Dot, do me a favor, please?"

"Depends." She smiled. "What?"

"You went running by yourself at night, in the winter?"

"Uh-huh."

He sighed. "Please be careful." His eyes were serious. "I know you can take care of yourself, but still…"

She laughed, flattered by his concern. "Boone, believe me, it can't happen often. I usually run when the boys are at practice, or I default to the treadmill."

"Okay." His smile returned, full force. "Anyway, I love the painting. How about I buy it when it's done? I'd love to have it for my new place when I move."

Dot turned toward the door and flashed him a smile over her shoulder. "We'll see."

Chapter Seven

It was New Year's Eve and Dot stood in front of her closet. This was stupid. Asinine, really. She was a grown woman, committed to not involving herself with a man until her boys had been launched in the world, and yet she had been digging through her closet for almost a half-hour. The party at Georgiana's that night wasn't a fancy event but deciding what to wear to a small get-together involving Chinese food, sledding, and watching the ball drop was taxing nonetheless.

Dot had been spending this evening at Georgiana's for the past six years and it had become a tradition her boys loved. This year was no different. She was making a big deal out of nothing.

But it wasn't nothing! No matter how much she told herself she was being an idiot, Boone was going to be there, and Georgiana now being fully committed to Jack meant that this New Year's Eve was different.

Ever since Thanksgiving, Boone had occupied her thoughts more than he should have. No matter how many times she told herself to remember that she didn't get involved with men in a romantic way, she had to admit she had thought about him a lot. An awful lot.

On Christmas, after the chaos was over and the boys were sprawled on the couch half-asleep from all the excitement, she had sat down in her favorite chair to knit for a while. Just then, her phone had buzzed. Looking down, she read, *Hi, Dot, just wanted to wish you and the guys a Merry Christmas. See you on New Year's!*

That text had made her so happy, it rattled her. She had felt special. Important. Eighteen words on a little screen had made her feel like a princess.

Dot shook her head, clearing thoughts of the text from her mind. It was time to focus on tonight's event at Georgiana's. Silly thoughts, some even irrational, zipped through her mind. Maybe she should stay home. She could say she didn't feel well but could still drop off the boys. Georgiana always loved to have them stay over, so that could work.

She stomped over to her bed and flopped on it, surrendering herself to the fact that backing out was not a viable plan. Georgiana would see right through her. And worse than that, she would hound Dot until she told her the reason behind the childish excuse. What the hell could she say? Without realizing what she was doing, she spoke aloud. "Yeah, George, I lied. I admit it. The thing is, I can't go because I have the hots for Boone even though I absolutely won't act on them. I can't behave like some giggly fourteen-year-old. Fuck!"

Just then, Finn poked his head around the corner. "Mom, you okay? You're talking to yourself, like really loud."

Dot laughed. "Yeah, Finn. I'm fine. Just being silly, that's all."

"Okay, just making sure." He rolled his eyes.

"Thanks, bud. I'll be down in ten minutes. Make sure your brother is ready, okay?"

Dot drove to the farm, barely listening as her boys chattered about the Bruins game they had watched that afternoon. She had finally settled on black jeans, a gray cowlneck sweater (that looked great with her hair), and her favorite winter jacket and hat. She was comfortable, looked appropriate for the event, and deep down, she knew she looked good.

She wasn't primping for Boone per se. (She swore she wasn't.) She was just going to a party with friends, and it wouldn't be right to not dress well for it. It would be disrespectful to her hosts, right?

"Mom! Are you listening to me?"

Shit! What had she missed? "Of course, I am, Dec. Why do you ask?"

"Because I just told you we think you look nice tonight, and you didn't say a word."

Her sons taking notice of her efforts melted her heart. She had raised good boys, even if it felt like she had winged it a hell of a lot. "Thanks, Dec. You're right, I was daydreaming, but I really appreciate the compliment."

When Dot and the boys arrived, Boone, Julia, and PJ were already there. With the small but boisterous group, they had all eaten Chinese food at the long dining room table. Then, with torches lighting the hillside, they sledded for hours. Just the memory made Dot hug herself happily. She knew deep down that she could not let anything happen with Boone, even if he was interested, but boy, it had been a lot of fun to flirt tonight. They had shared a sled, pelted each other with snowballs, and hugged at midnight. It had almost felt like a date.

Hours later, she guided her sleepy boys into their bedroom. "You can sleep in your clothes. Forget your teeth for tonight." They muttered their agreement and headed toward their room as she let Atticus out for his last pee break.

She tucked the boys into their beds, even if they were a little old for it, and leaned down to kiss each of them. She turned off the lights and closed their door on her way out. Atticus was at the top step, ready to come in and follow her to her bedroom. Great, her bedmate was a Basset Hound. One who had to be hoisted onto the bed each night, no less. Her social life was pathetic.

Dot changed into her pajamas, then sat at the window seat and looked out over the fields. She was too wound up to sleep, no matter how late the hour. It had been a perfect night, and she wanted to relive every moment. With a disgruntled sigh because he was alone in bed, Atticus curled up on the quilt and was soon snoring softly as Dot reminisced on the evening.

Her phone buzzed. *Hey, I had a great time tonight. Sorry if this weirds you out, but is it okay if I text you occasionally?*

Dot almost jumped out of her skin. Boone wanted to text her. That was more than her brain could handle.

She had to think about this. *Was* it okay to text with him? Would it just be for fun, or was that going too far? Was she leading him on? She decided it didn't matter at that moment. *That would be awesome.*

Great, then Happy New Year! Looking forward to being your neighbor soon. Good night.

Good night — Happy New Year!

Chapter Eight

Dot glared at herself in the mirror. She had let herself get lulled into routine texting with Boone over the past three months. Silly texts, and several a day. Getting-to-know-you texts, she justified. (Edging on flirtatious if she was being honest.) And now he was officially moving to town, and she didn't have the foggiest clue what to do. She couldn't date anyone. Not that he had asked her out, but if he did, she knew she would need to decline.

She sat on the edge of her bed, head in her hands. It had been a long, lonely eight years since Mike died. Mike. Her Mike. Her first boyfriend and her husband. She leaned over and studied his picture on the bedside table. Their first date had been on her sixteenth birthday, bowling. They married at eighteen, worked day and night, and bought this house with the money they had scraped together. Dreams of owning his own construction company while she became a successful painter drove them to work much of the time. Then they started a family.

It had been wonderful; Mike was a great husband and father. They had been so happy before it was all was shattered the day of the car accident. Her husband was gone, leaving her a widow and a single parent.

Dot stroked his photographed face. She had been lost for months after he died. Had it not been for Georgiana, she probably would have lost the house; grief-stricken, she had not paid bills for months. Once she got her head relatively straight again, she swore she would never let her boys struggle without her. She would devote every minute of her life to keeping them safe and happy.

That was when she swore she would stay away from men until the boys were on their own, or at least in college. They needed a full-time parent, that was for certain.

She had only slipped up once in all these years, compromising her personal vow. The boys had a hockey clinic in Montreal, and she had stayed in a nearby hotel, just in case they needed her. She went to a local hockey bar that night, and after a few drinks she found herself in bed with a young man, an energetic but dull lover. She scurried out of the room and made a shameful retreat to her hotel.

That had been a one-time thing. She could not deny she missed having a man in her life. Hell, she really missed the sex, but the boys were her focus. So now that Boone was in town, she needed to figure out how to ease up on the gas pedal. The texting had been fun, a thrill really. Their exchanges were sexy as hell, but she needed to keep things in perspective. She likened this to the once or twice a year she allowed herself a piece of tiramisu; it was deliciously forbidden, but not in her best interest as a matter of habit.

Fuck!

Now she needed to make sure she behaved herself. She was going to need a lot of cold showers. On second thought, maybe a better vibrator. Maybe both...

Chapter Nine

Two days later, Dot's phone buzzed as she unloaded groceries. It was a text from Boone. *Hey, want to see my new house? And how about I buy that painting now?*

Did she want to see him? Hell, yes. Should she see him? Hell, no. But that would be rude, wouldn't it? She looked to the corner of the living room where the neatly wrapped package leaned against the wall. She had finished the painting weeks ago and once the paint cured, she had wrapped it as a housewarming gift for Boone. If she hurried with putting the groceries away, she could stop by to see him before collecting the boys from the rink. It would be nothing more than a friendly drop-in to say hello. It had nothing to do with her wanting to see that gorgeous, sexy man. That was the neighborly thing to do, right? Nothing more.

Yeah, right. As Georgiana would say, it was time to call bullshit.

A half-hour later, Dot pulled into the driveway. Boone was now renting Jack's old house, and it already looked so different. He had hung curtains in the windows and placed some nice rocking chairs on the front porch. Hmmm, the Navy SEAL hung curtains and decorated. Fascinating.

She parked by the garage and jumped out, refusing to indulge her inclination to take one more look in the mirror. This was no big deal, she reminded herself, so there was no reason to check her appearance again.

Opening the hatchback, she pulled out the package and did her best to hide it behind her as she approached the house.

She was just about to ring the doorbell when Boone opened the door. "Dot, I'm so glad to see you. Come on in."

Jesus H. Christ! He was in jeans and a t-shirt that fit like a second skin. No matter how much she wanted to deny it, this man did things to her. She stepped into the foyer and pulled the package from behind her. "Surprise! Happy Housewarming!"

His eyes widened. "No way!"

"Yes," she nodded. "Open it."

Boone took the package from her and gingerly pushed the wrapping aside. "It's amazing," he gasped. "Dot, I love it. It's great." His eyes met hers. "But please, let me buy it. This has value, you should get paid for your time."

She shook her head and chuckled. "No, Boone. It's either a gift, or I take it back home. I paint for my friends because I want to. It's a gift, simple as that."

She could see how touched he was. "Thanks, Dot. I really do love it." Putting it down to lean against a side table in the hall, he opened his arms and hugged her. "Thank you."

He smelled so good. Clean. Masculine. Almost spicy. It was a fragrance she could imagine taking in for the rest of her days. Dot reciprocated the hug quickly, knowing she needed to break physical contact before she broke her self-imposed rules of purity. "You're so welcome," she said. "Happy housewarming!"

"Home." He grinned. "I like that." He tipped his head, clearly thinking. "I've moved from one base to another for so many years, it seems odd to know I can stay for good."

Dot was interested in this thought. "And is that a good thing?"

"It is." He gestured with one hand. "Come on, let me give you the tour, and you can help me decide where to display the painting."

Chapter Ten

A month later, Dot knew she was in over her head, and yet, she couldn't really figure out how to stop. It was like Halloween candy. She could restrain herself most of the year, but after the boys trick-or-treated and snagged their favorites, she usually found herself eating the leftovers, no matter how many times she told herself to stop. The next day always involved a sugar hangover followed by Georgiana giving her shit for it, but she still did it.

Boone was like that basket of candy. She needed to stop, she knew that in her bones, but she couldn't. She was careful to keep it platonic, like buddies, but it was getting hard to limit it to that. Each text gave her the same rush as one of those mini candy bars, and then she would beat herself up for feeling that way. Even so, she anticipated the buzz of her phone.

Wait. Maybe she was reading too far into it. Maybe Boone was just looking for a friend too. Yes, he texted her every day, but he had never asked her out. They laughed, they exchanged silly texts, but that was it. If he wanted something more, it would have happened by now, right?

She needed to stay the course. She could be friends with him, even text with him, but that was it. No matter how hot he was, she was not getting involved with a man until her boys were launched-that was her plan and what she had promised in honor of Mike's memory.

Shit, if only Boone wasn't so tempting.

Standing among garage doors at Home Depot, Dot checked her phone. What the hell was that thing called again? Door gasket, that was it. She needed a vinyl garage door gasket. Now, where would that be?

Scrolling through the store's website, she realized that if they had it, it would be on an end cap. With a huff, she turned to the end of the aisle.

Black. Brown. Where was the white? She needed white, and the website said they had it. She glanced over her shoulder to look for an employee, but as was usually the case in this store, there wasn't one to be found. Just then, she caught sight of something white, but it was out of her reach. Being only five-foot three, most things were out of her reach, but she had learned to adapt over the years. If they were going to place merchandise that high and not have employees around, she would have to take matters into her own hands.

Standing on the shelf below, she worked to balance herself while stretching as high as she could.

Just as her fingertips reached the item, firm hands grasped her waist, and a familiar voice said, "Well, if this isn't the best sight I've ever seen in a Home Depot." He wrapped one arm around her waist, easing her down. "And get the hell off the shelves before you hurt yourself."

Her feet now on the floor, Dot squeaked, "Boone! Knock it off, I almost had it!" She swatted at him playfully.

He rolled his eyes. "I'll get it for you, but I will not watch you pull things down on yourself, sweetheart, or fall and hurt yourself."

Sweetheart? What the hell did that mean? She tried to regain her composure. "Fine." She softened her tone. "I want the white vinyl door gasket, an eight-foot strip."

With seemingly no effort at all, Boone raised his arm over his head and pulled down the item. "Here you go."

"Thank you."

He looked in her cart. "So, fixing the garage door and a faucet. Want help?"

She should say no. The hard part would be to say no and really mean it. "That would be great." The words seemed to tumble out of her mouth before she knew it.

"Cool." He picked his small basket up from the floor. "Are you ready?"

"I am."

Dot talked to herself the whole way home, Boone driving right behind her. "Don't be stupid, Dot. Don't. He's hotter than hell, a nice guy, funny, sexy, smart, and seems like he's interested. And all of that doesn't matter because you don't date. The boys need you. If you get involved with Boone, or any other guy for that matter, the boys could feel like they've lost another parent. They are your first responsibility." She beat her hands on the steering wheel for emphasis and straightened her posture as if to instill some extra confidence in herself. "Remember that, Dot," she said as she pulled up to the house.

As she got out of the car, Boone appeared. "Tools still in the same place?"

"They are."

"I'll work on the garage door while there's still light, then come in for the faucet."

She looked at him for a moment, trying to figure out what to do. Finally, she said, "What do I owe you?"

"You don't owe me anything," he said, "it is my pleasure."

"Then how about dinner? The boys are with friends tonight, so I was going to grill up a nice steak. Please, Boone, you have to let me thank you somehow."

His smile gave her a rush of unexpected joy. "I would love a homecooked meal."

"Good. I'll get started. You know where to find me if you need anything."

The next afternoon, Boone stood in his kitchen wondering what to do. Normally, he would have just asked her out the night before, but with Dot, everything was different. The dinner had been fabulous, and they had shared a good bottle of wine. They talked for hours. They laughed. Even doing the dishes had been fun. It had been a great evening, and he wanted to spend more time with her. Who was he kidding? He wanted to spend *all* his time with her.

What should he do? He knew Georgiana said Dot did not date because she was a mother first and foremost, but everything in him felt the interest was mutual. Should he ask her out? If so, how? Call? Text? Stop by her house? No, the house was out. The boys could be home, and he did not want to put her in an awkward position. So, he should call? No, then she would feel like she had been put on the spot. Texting was the right answer. They texted all the time, and she seemed comfortable with that. He could ask, she could think about it, and hopefully she would say yes.

He typed and retyped until he felt he got it right.

Hi Dot, thanks for dinner last night, it was great. I was wondering if you'd like to go out sometime.

When two hours passed without an answer, Boone's heart sank. Clearly, he had misinterpreted their interactions. Annoyed with himself, and disappointed, he threw on some running clothes and headed out the door to work off this bad energy, leaving his phone behind.

An hour later, tired but more relaxed, Boone arrived home to find he had a voicemail. "Hi Boone, it's Dot. Sorry to leave you a message, I thought I would reach you by calling. I got your text. Thank you so, so much for the invitation, but... Boone, it's not that I don't want to go out with you, it's... Well, it's that I don't date. I haven't dated anyone since Mike died, and I vowed I wouldn't date until the boys are older." She laughed, sounding uncomfortable. "Hopefully someone will still be interested in me then. But anyway, thank you, and I hope you can understand, and that we can still be friends and hang out. Bye."

Shit.

Chapter Eleven

A month later, Julia left to visit her parents, so Georgiana invited PJ and Boone to dinner. Jack had greeted them at the door and the three men went to do chores in the barn while Georgiana was busy in the kitchen.

About thirty minutes later, the trio could be heard entering the mudroom. Georgiana was struck by the exasperation in her brother's voice. "Seriously, man, what the hell is your problem tonight? You're just an ass today."

Boone's voice shot back defensively, "I am not."

"Boone, PJ's right," said Jack. "What's going on? You've snapped at us both in the last five minutes alone." After all the time they had been together, Georgiana still felt a rush of love whenever she heard her fiancé's voice.

Boone sat down at the kitchen table with a harrumph. "I'm fine. Just cranky, I guess."

Jack opened the fridge and pulled out three beers, giving one to each of the men. "Babe, you want anything?"

She shook her head. "Not right now, thanks."

PJ shifted his attention back to Boone. "Why are you cranky?"

"I don't know, I just am."

Georgiana stood at the sink, her back to the group as she peeled carrots. "Has nothing to do with a lack of social life, does it?"

Boone's voice immediately rose. "What the hell does that mean?"

Georgiana knew she had hit a nerve, but she was completely comfortable with moody men. "Your crankiness might have something to do with the fact that you haven't had a date since you moved here."

PJ and Jack both looked at Boone. His face darkened with anger. PJ took a swig, then said, "Is she right?"

Boone slammed his bottle down on the table, making everyone jump, and slopping a little beer on the table. "Yes, of course she's right." Boone rolled his eyes. "Gigi is always right; don't we all know that by now?"

Jack handed him a napkin. "So, ask someone out already. Damn, it's not like there aren't at least a few single women around."

Georgiana jumped in before Boone could respond. "He asked someone out, he's just pissy that she didn't say yes."

"God damn it, Gi! Stay the fuck out of my business," Boone yelled.

She turned around, drying her hands on a towel. "I'm not interfering in your business. I'm just explaining why you are being such an asshole, that's all."

Boone glared at her. "Then tell me what to do, Gi."

PJ shook his head. He was used to the two of them fighting like this. "Okay, stop for a second. Who did you ask out, and why did she decline?"

Boone looked at Georgiana. "You going to let me tell them, or are you going to?"

She shrugged. "You can."

Boone took a sip. "I asked Dot out a month ago."

This was news to PJ. "You did? And you didn't say anything?"

"No, I didn't. Sometimes I get to have a private life, you know."

PJ tried to hide his smirk. "Continue…"

Boone sighed. "We hung out a couple times and I helped her with some stuff around the house. We were texting each other since Thanksgiving, stuff like that. I thought she was interested, so I asked her out."

"And?" said Jack.

"And it seemed like she liked me, so I asked her out via text, thinking it would be less awkward than face to face."

"And?"

"And she left me a voicemail saying she really appreciated the thought, but she doesn't date. Not like, not now… Like never, or at least until the boys are grown. Like, forget about it. Done."

PJ looked at his friend. "And you don't want it to be done?"

Boone shook his head and shrugged. "No, I don't. I really like her. And I would like to see if things could go somewhere, but she clearly doesn't feel the same way."

Before either man could say anything, Georgiana turned around, smiling. "Boonie, I don't think that's really it."

"What do you mean?"

"I don't think it's that she doesn't like you or want to date you."

"Well, if you're right, she has a strange way of showing it," he grumbled.

Georgiana nodded. "I know it sounds weird, but I think she's scared."

"Scared?" all three men chorused.

"Yes," she nodded.

Boone was confused. "Of what? How did I scare her?"

Georgiana sat down and Jack watched in amusement as she leaned forward with her elbows on the table, like she did when she was really concentrating on a conversation. "You didn't scare her. The idea of dating someone scares her."

"She was married. How can she be afraid of dating?"

"That's just it. She was married for years, then widowed. Shit, Boonie, she met Mike at sixteen, and that was it. I don't think she ever even dated anyone before him. Then he was killed. And she hasn't dated anyone since. No one. And it's not that she hasn't been asked, she just refuses."

"Why?"

"Because she's still struggling with whether she's still married, and because she made a commitment to put the boys first, no matter what."

PJ looked at his sister like she was insane. "Mike's been dead for almost eight years. I don't see the issue."

"The issue is that she married him for her life, not just his. She doesn't believe his death changed their commitment to each other, and she feels like she needs to show the boys she loved their dad. She also feels, unequivocally, that the boys always need to come first and that they need to know it."

Boone was sitting silently, but PJ continued. "That's stupid."

"No, it isn't," said Jack. "It makes sense the way Gia explains it." He looked at Boone. "Sorry, Boone. It seems like you're out of luck on this one."

Georgiana jumped in, "I didn't say that. I only explained why she turned him down. I didn't say he should give up."

Boone shook his head. "Jesus, Gi. Now I am completely confused."

"Look, Boone, I know Dot has been asked out over the years. Angus asked her out about five years ago, and I know that to be a fact. The thing is, she never talked about it. He told me, not her. But in your case, she told me you asked her out. That's an enormous difference. Especially since you and I once dated. I would have thought she might avoid confiding in me. So, you see, if there was no hope, I would never have known a thing."

Boone pondered that thought, then finally spoke. "Okay, so if that's the case, what the heck am I supposed to do?"

"You let her set the pace. She said she wants to be friends and still hang out with you. So do that. Don't ask her out, don't bring her flowers, don't hold her hand. Keep it like you were hanging out with these guys. Let her get to a point where she feels safe enough to consider going out with you. Stick around long enough, safely enough, that she gets to a point where she can't stand the idea of missing out on you."

Boone took Georgiana's advice. A week after that conversation, he sat at his kitchen counter, trying to craft a text.

Hey, it's me. I was wondering if you were bored enough that you'd be interested in me bringing a movie over on Friday night? I'll even bring the popcorn.

Minutes later, his phone buzzed, and as he turned it over, he smiled.

Sounds great. You bring the movie, I'll make calzones. 5:30?

Chapter Twelve

Over the next months, they settled into an easy routine. On Fridays, Boone had dinner with Dot and the boys, and they watched a movie. Some nights he brought takeout; some nights she cooked, or they all cooked together. No matter how much he wanted to move Dot toward being a couple, he kept his word, allowing things to progress at her pace.

One Friday night in early December, he knocked on the door. Dot opened it, drying her hands on her jeans. Before she could stop it, she could feel herself blush as he came in. "Hey."

"Hey." His arms were full, but his smile was wide as he looked at her. "I got the sandwiches and everything."

"Thank you."

After dinner, they all settled in the living room. Dot took to her favorite rocking chair, her bare feet up on the coffee table. She knew she shouldn't sit on the couch with Boone, after all, she needed to keep this strictly platonic, with absolutely no room for misunderstandings.

As the night went on, she let her mind wander in the darkened room, glad Boone and the boys were focused on the hockey movie. She rocked in the chair, wondering what the hell she was doing with her life. Here she was, a widow, having a weekly dinner and movie with the most beautiful man she knew.

She snuck a look at him. Tall, with jet black hair, still cut very short. Muscles everywhere, rock hard muscles, but not freakish. That dimple in his left cheek when he smiled. Big hands that petted old Atticus so gently. He was fucking amazing. Gorgeous, sweet, sexy, funny, and smart. He had her brain and her hormones in a complete tizzy. So, each Friday, they had a standing dinner and a movie, and she spent all week looking forward to these few hours.

What else did she like about him? He was opinionated and didn't worry about always agreeing with her. Sometimes he was a bit chauvinistic, thinking she was too delicate to do things like carry a bag of dog food. She always had to prove that she could do things for herself, but deep down, she had to admit that she liked how he wanted to help her.

His flaws? He loved marshmallows. Yuck. Dot hated marshmallows with a passion, and Boone could eat an entire bag in one sitting. He loved disco music, and Dot would rather listen to Atticus howl. He loved the Dallas Cowboys, and she was a Patriots fan. He insisted on untying his shoes every time he took them off, while Dot tended to just slip them on and off, still tied.

They were together every Friday night, yet they were not a couple. Ever since that horribly awkward voicemail when she had told him they couldn't go out, it seemed as if he wasn't interested in her anymore. Had he friend-zoned her? Well, that was what she wanted, right? With a quiet sigh, she found herself rocking faster in her chair. Why the heck hadn't she said yes to going on a date with him? How long was he going to be content with these Friday nights? How was she going to feel when he got bored with this, and stopped coming over because he was dating someone else? Without realizing it, she shook her head.

Boone's voice came out of the darkness, sounding concerned. "Dot, you okay?"

"What do you mean?"

Dec laughed. "Mom, you rocked, then you sighed, then you made a snorty sound and shook your head. You talking to yourself again?"

Crap! She needed to keep her romantic thoughts in check. "No, I'm not talking to myself. Just thinking about what I need to do tomorrow."

Boone eyed her suspiciously. "Okay."

Two hours later, as the credits rolled, Boone stood up and snagged the cookie bag and the almost empty bag of chips. "Come on, guys, help me clean up."

Dot followed them all out to the kitchen, then sent the boys out. "Guys, take Atticus out to pee." She rolled her eyes, knowing how they normally did things. "And wait outside until he's done his business."

She looked out the kitchen window, suddenly realizing that Boone's truck glistened in the moonlight, completely covered in a sheet of ice. "Oh my gosh, it's sleeting like hell out there."

He came over to stand next to her. "It is. I guess we missed that."

No matter how much she wanted to keep things simple, she hated the idea of him driving in such weather. "Do you want to stay? You can sleep on the couch."

He shook his head. "Nah, Dot. Thanks for the offer. It's only two miles home. I'll be fine, I'll take it real slow." He chuckled, nudging her with his elbow. "Keep in mind, I trained for driving in combat. A little sleet doesn't worry me."

They were startled as Declan burst through the door, letting go of the leash. As the dog padded into the warmth of the house, the boy stood frozen in the doorway, his voice panicked. "Mom! Finn is hurt, bad!"

Later, Dot would realize that the next seconds felt like hours. Fear filled her as she lurched for the door in time for Finn to appear, blood gushing from his left arm. (She would later see the absurdity in her first thought: Why had he gone out without a coat?)

Finn looked shocked. He silently held out his arm, one hand half covering the wound on his bare arm. Dot took one look at her son, her baby boy, and she felt the world spin. There was so much blood.

Boone took one look at Dot's sickly green complexion and shoved her into a chair. "Sit. Now," he said.

She struggled to stand up again, pushing against his hand. "No. I need to take care of Finn. I need to get him to the emergency room."

"Sit your ass down," he barked. "That's an order." He grabbed a dish towel. "Finn, sit down, bud. Sit in the chair next to your mom. It's okay, I've got this."

Dot raised her voice. "No, Boone, I need to take him to the ER!"

He would later wonder why she did not react to his choice of words: "Baby, listen to me. The roads are too dangerous for that. We need to deal with this here. I've got this, okay?"

Dot stood up, compelled to help her son. Her voice rose. "Boone, he's going to need stitches," she exclaimed.

"Dot, sit your goddamn ass down and listen to me." She sat next to Finn, nearly toppling the chair as she obeyed him.

Boone's voice softened as he pulled the boy's arm closer, placing it on a towel he had spread on the table. "Finn, I need to get a good look at this, okay?

All you need to do is sit still, breathe, and we will take care of this in no time."

Finn's voice shook, "Boone, you know what to do?"

Boone calmly assessed the situation. "Dude, I was a SEAL medic. Yeah, I know what to do." He grinned and winked at the terrified boy, exuding confidence. "I mean, it's not as much fun as a bullet wound, but I can still take care of it."

Bullet wounds? Now he had Finn's interest. "Really? You took care of someone who got shot?"

"Yeah, I did." Pulling one hand off the wound, Boone rested the back of his hand on the boy's face. "I've dealt with a lot of bullet wounds. I'll tell you all about them sometime." He needed to get the boy's fear under control. "Really, Finn. I've got this. You just do as I say, okay? You trust me, don't you?"

The boy nodded as Boone placed a tourniquet made from a towel around Finn's upper arm. "Hey, Dec?"

Declan was standing behind Boone, his eyes wide with fear. "Yeah?"

"Buddy, I need your help, okay?" Boone kept his eyes on the wound in front of him. His voice reflected the fact that he was in complete control. "You able to be my second in command?"

Declan's voice trembled. "I am."

"Good." He took a quick look at Declan, noting how pale he was. "I need you to go, carefully, out to my truck. It's unlocked, but you saw how icy it is out there, so take it easy, okay? Are you listening?"

The boy focused on Boone's face, not wanting to disappoint him. "I'm listening." Declan looked down at the dog sitting at Finn's feet, watching everything with his sad eyes.

"And leave Atticus here," said Boone.

Dot could not contain herself much longer. "How did this happen anyway?" she blurted.

Boone spoke over her. "Dot, we can figure that out later. Dec, in the back seat of my truck, behind the driver's seat, there is a big black bag."

The boy nodded. "Big black bag in the back seat."

"You got it. That's my medic bag. I need you to go out, being wicked careful on the ice, and bring it to me. Okay?"

"Black bag. Careful. I've got it."

Boone nodded. "Go get it. We're okay here, but I need that bag right away."

"I'm on it."

"That's my man. Now go," he urged.

Less than a minute later, Declan came in, struggling with the weight of the bag. Keeping his eyes locked on Finn's, Boone said, "Okay, Dec, open the bag for me?" Finn's breathing was shallow but regular, and Boone was happy to see some color returning to the boy's cheeks. The shock was subsiding, which was a good thing.

"Okay."

"In the side pocket, there is a large, blue, square packet. See it?"

Declan dug around. "Here, you mean this?"

"Yes, take that out and put it on the table, but don't open it yet. That's a sterile pad that I'm going to use to keep Finn safe."

"Done."

"Good." Boone smiled. "Now go wash your hands really well. Soap them up good and rinse them carefully. And dry them with paper towels, okay? Not the dish towels."

"Got it," said Declan. A minute later, he was back at Boone's side. "Done."

"Now I want you to open the packet for me, then unfold the pad. When I tell you, I'm going to have you slide it under Finn's arm, got it?"

"Got it."

"Okay, now…"

Without a word, Dec slid the pad under his brother's arm. "Good job. Now, buddy, you able to help me some more?".

"Yeah, I'm okay, Boone." Declan stood a little straighter under the weight of what he knew to be an important assignment.

Boone smiled, knowing how scared both boys must be. "Okay, here's the deal, you have a super important job now."

"Okay."

"When I tell you, your hands will quickly replace mine here, and you are going to press firmly, but not too hard, while I get cleaned up. I know it's a little gross, but I know you can do it."

"Okay, I got it."

Boone detected a tremor in the boy's determined voice, and his heart swelled. "That's outstanding, Dec. Isn't that outstanding, Finn?"

The little boy tried to smile, his face streaked with tears. "Yeah, thanks, Dec."

"Remind me sometime to tell you all about the time I had to fix up PJ's butt after he took a bullet there, okay?"

Both boys looked more relaxed. Declan giggled. "Really? He got shot in the butt?"

"He did." Boone looked at Dec. "Alright, let's do this."

While Boone washed up, Dot kissed Finn's temple. "Someone want to tell me what the heck happened out there?"

Dec was holding onto the wound with both hands, trying not to look at the blood still seeping through his fingers. "We were trying to get icicles to have a sword fight. You know, where they hang really long by the garage."

Dot nodded. "I do."

Finn's voice wavered. "I climbed up on the railing…"

"And?"

Dec bit his lip, then seemed to steel himself, ready to brave her anger. "I poked at Finn with my sword, and he fell off the railing and caught his arm on the post on the chicken coop."

Boone was just coming back from the sink. "Metal post?"

Dot nodded. "Yes."

"When was his last tetanus shot?"

It helped clear away her fear to think of a fact like that. "Last month, at his physical."

"Good." He smiled at the boys. "Mom can chew you out later about being on the railing and all that, but right now, let's do this."

A half hour later, Finn's wound was clean and closed with a combination of Steri-Strips and skin glue. Boone's gloved hand gave Finn a pat. "You were lucky, little man. It bled like crazy, but that's because you not only got a nasty puncture wound, but one heck of a scrape too. Believe it or not, that's what bled most."

"Oh."

Once the arm was bandaged, Boone reached into his kit one more time, retrieving a black cloth. "Okay, buddy, this is the last step. Mom is going to get you some Tylenol to help with the pain, and I'm going to have your brother help me wrap this ice blanket around your arm for the night."

When everything was done, Boone smiled down at his exhausted patient. "Finn, dude, you were amazing. I've seen soldiers not half as brave as you. You did a magnificent job."

Finn looked up at him with surprise. "Really?"

Boone squatted down, so they were eye to eye. "Really, buddy." He looked at the older brother. "The two of you were rock stars." Before Dot came back, he whispered, "Your mom needed you both to be strong, and you did it like champs."

Finn smiled, putting his good arm around Boone's neck in a tight hug. "Thanks, Boone, for fixing me up."

"My pleasure, dude. Now I'm going to carry you into the living room, even though I know you can walk. I just want you to stay quiet, okay? Dec will be in to watch TV with you once he gets cleaned up."

Once he was sure the boys were settled, Boone returned to the kitchen and was startled to find Dot staring out the kitchen window. She seemed mesmerized by the sleet. "Dot?"

She didn't reply. Without thinking about what he was doing, he placed his hands gently on her shoulders. "He's okay, Dot. He's going to be fine. Tomorrow you can take him to his doctor to be checked out, but he's going to be just fine."

She turned to him, and he realized how pale she had become. "He's okay only because you were here."

"What do you mean?"

"I froze, Boone. I fucking froze."

Boone shook his head. "You didn't freeze. You were ready to take him to the ER, but we were able to handle it here instead of risking the trip in this weather. You all did what I needed you to do, and we worked as a team."

Tears pooled in her eyes. "Thank you."

"For what?"

She reached out and gave him a fierce, spontaneous hug. "You saved him. You took control of the situation, you took care of him, and you made both boys feel strong while you did it."

He rested his chin on the top of her head. He loved the feeling of finally holding her in his arms. "We all have our areas of expertise. I know how to take care of a wound, and I know how to distract people."

She started to laugh but maintained their embrace. "You made them laugh while you patched him up."

He chuckled. "Yeah, PJ is going to love that they know he has a scar on his ass, but you do what it takes to keep a kid calm."

She leaned back to look up at him, then stretched up and kissed him gently on the cheek. "Thank you."

"You're welcome."

She stepped back and looked down at the floor sheepishly. "Will you please stay the night?"

He shook his head. "Dot, I'll be fine. I will take it really slow."

"Please, Boone," her voice cracked. "Please stay. I really don't want you driving in this and..."

"And?"

"And I'm worried that Finn's arm could open up. If you're here, maybe I won't be scared."

He knew this had to be hard for her to say. This was a woman who hated to admit she needed help from anyone. "Ah, so you finally admit I can be helpful sometimes."

She laughed. "Yes, I admit it."

He grinned. "I'll stay. I can sleep on the couch once the boys go to bed, and if Finn needs anything, he can give me a shout."

Neither of them realized that Declan had walked into the kitchen. "Boone?" he said.

"Oh, hey, bud." Boone smiled.

"You could stay in our room. You can sleep in my bed, and I can sleep on the floor. That way, well, you'd be right there."

Boone looked at the tired boy. "I'll make a deal with you. Go throw your sleeping bag on the floor in your room. I'll sleep there, while you guys keep your beds. If either of you need anything, you just ask."

The boy spun around without another word to the adults. "Finn, Boone is going to have a sleepover with us!"

Fifteen minutes later, Dot hid a smile as she entered the boys' room. Her sons were in their normal spots and Boone was stretched out on the floor in a sleeping bag atop a stack of quilts. As she did every night, she tucked the boys in and kissed them goodnight before turning toward the door.

"Night, guys. Go to sleep." She grinned down at Boone. "That means all three of you."

Finn looked at his brother mischievously. "Mom, you didn't kiss Boone."

"Silly me, what was I thinking," she said sarcastically. The boys giggled as she made a display of theatrically creeping over to the sleeping bag. She steadied herself with a hand on the floor and leaned over, kissing Boone's forehead with a loud, dramatic smooch that had them all giggling. "Sweet dreams, Boone," she chuckled.

Sweet dreams, indeed.

The next morning, Dot awoke nervous and exhausted. She had tossed and turned half the night, wondering if Finn was okay, and thinking about Boone. No man had stayed overnight in her house since Mike died, and to have Boone sleeping in the boys' room felt… funny. Standing in front of her dresser mirror, she buttoned the faded flannel shirt, knowing the colors looked good on her and the soft fabric draped nicely over her curves.

What the hell was she doing worrying about how her boobs looked in this shirt? She had told Boone no. It was simpler that way, no complications. She was a mother, first and foremost. The boys had lost their dad, they needed her to be their rock. Dating was out of the question until they were grown and on their own. It had to be this way, right?

She sat down and pulled on some woolly socks. She had made her decision long ago; she would never try juggling a man and her boys. That was the right decision, wasn't it?

She thought back to all the times Georgiana had argued that children were better off with two parents, and better adjusted if their parents were happy. This was advice from a woman who was not only raised without a dad but had also lived away from her mother for years. What did Georgiana know about normal households?

Would it really be so bad if the boys saw her go out on an occasional date? They liked Boone, that was clear.

Dot opened the bedroom door with a sigh. The smell of coffee was intoxicating. Boone must have already gotten a jump on the day. How thoughtful.

Pressing her lips together to bring some color to them, she strode down the hall and stairs, suddenly looking forward to sitting with Boone for that first cup of coffee.

She stopped short as she entered the kitchen. There was a note on the counter, her favorite mug holding it in place.

Morning Dot,

I had to get to work early, but I got the coffee going for you. I hope I didn't wake you up.

Let me know how it goes with Finn's doctor and keep me posted as to how he's doing.

Thanks for letting me crash last night.
Boone

Dammit! She had genuinely wanted to sit and have coffee, just the two of them, and now he was gone.

Two hours later, she returned home, glad to see the plow guy had sanded her driveway. She sent the boys into the house while she sat in the car to text Boone.

Hey, doc says you did a great job. Nothing was broken, nothing needed stitching, just a really bad cut. He said F's arm will heal well, probably w/o a scar, to his disappointment. Thanks so much. Want to come to dinner tonight?

Sitting at the kitchen table at Jack and Georgiana's house, Boone read the text. Georgiana craned her neck to see it. "What does it say?"

"She says Finn is going to be fine."

"And?"

"And she asked me to come to dinner."

Jack noted the look on his face. "And?"

"And I can't go."

"Why not?"

"Because I can't do this anymore."

"Do what?"

"Be nothing more than her buddy." He looked at Georgiana sadly. "I tried, Gi, I really did. I followed your advice. I didn't push, I just hung out with her, with the boys, like we were just friends, nothing more. But last night, after Finn's accident, she initiated a hug, and then she kissed my cheek. And frankly, even with what we had just been through, I didn't react like we were just buddies. I want her. It was all I could do to not wrap her in my arms and kiss her senseless. I want to be in a legitimate relationship with her and I don't want to be just friends." He gave the table a sharp rap with his hand, as if to emphasize his point. "I cannot keep pretending I'm okay with this."

Georgiana saw the pain on his face. "What are you saying?" she said softly.

"I'm saying…" He paused. "Shit, I need to end it now."

"Boone…"

"No, Georgie. I love you and I appreciate your advice on this, but I tried it your way. Ever since that hug in her kitchen, it's like all bets are off and I can't go back. I also can't go to dinner as if I don't feel something, like I'm not attracted to her. I can be patient but I'm not a masochist." With that, Boone picked up his phone and quickly typed something until the telltale sound signified a message had been sent.

Dot's phone buzzed. The message was brief.

That's great news. And thanks for the invite but have to pass on dinner.

Chapter Thirteen

Two days passed without any word from Boone. Dot thought about calling Georgiana for advice but wondered if that would be weird. He and Georgiana had been an item, after all. But this was the first time she hadn't heard from Boone daily since they began texting months ago. She busied herself with household chores but continued to weigh whether calling would be helpful. Then again, why would Dot ask Georgiana anything if she had no intention of dating Boone? If they were keeping things platonic, she could wait to hear what he's been up to, right? But maybe a quick text to say hi was appropriate.

No matter the situation, Dot always weighed her options. She was standing at the gas station when she felt the urge to pull out her phone.

Hey, how's your week?

Boone was just pulling into his garage when he got Dot's text. He fought the little spark of happiness it gave him. But what the hell was she doing? Were they friends, or more than friends? For just a moment he let himself feel hope before reality washed over him. She had made it damn clear that she wasn't going to date him; all she wanted was a friend, and he didn't want to limit their relationship. He thought back to holding her in his arms, how perfectly she fit against him. Her hair had smelled so damn good, and he loved the feel of her lips on his cheek. Jesus, he was in over his head. It wasn't like he had lived his life as a monk, but this was so much more than he had ever felt before. This wasn't just about sex, although God knew how much he wanted her. This was about wanting to be with her day and night, touching her, becoming a presence in her life, and maybe even making a life together.

Holy crap. He was thinking about wanting a life with a woman he hadn't even kissed. Shit. He had it bad.

Getting out of the truck, he slammed the door harder than he intended. He stalked into the kitchen and dropped his phone on the counter. He wasn't going to do anything right this second.

As he unpacked his groceries, he speed-dialed Georgiana and placed the call on speaker phone. She picked up on the second ring. "Hey."

"Hey."

"You okay?"

He smiled; she knew him so well. "No."

"What's the matter?"

"Dot."

"What about Dot?"

"She doesn't want to date me but then she sends me texts asking about my week. I'm confused and I don't know what the heck she wants from me."

"You want me to talk to her?"

"No!" he shouted. He took a deep breath. "No, George. Thanks, but no. I don't know how to respond."

"Then ask her."

"I can't. I just need to respond cordially but briefly. I can't engage any more than that and I plan on not seeing her for a while until my feelings cool down. That's what I need to do."

"Boone." He could hear something going on in the background, then Georgiana continued. "Jack says hi and he wants to talk to you, but I said no. Boone, you've never felt like this about a woman before. Don't give up so easily. Ride it out and see where it goes."

"George, I *really* like her." He took a deep breath, then whispered, "I think I could fall in love with her. That's how much I feel for her, and I can't stand just being around her when there is little chance that's going to change." Before she could reply, Boone hurriedly said, "Gotta go, love you," and hung up.

He looked at his phone. Should he answer her text? To ignore it was rude, but he needed to keep it short and simple.

Good, thanks.

Then he turned off his phone.

Dot was shocked by the brevity of Boone's message. That was it? She scrolled back through her text history. They had volleyed all kinds of messages for months on end – long ones, silly ones, emojis, and gifs. Now he was sending her just two words? Worse yet, there was nothing here for her to respond to. She wondered if she had offended him in some way. With a huff, she texted him back.

Your fingers broken or something? Your texts are abruptly brief.

When no reply came in the next hour, Dot began to pace. Thankfully, the boys were at a hockey training camp for the afternoon, so they didn't see her acting like a crazy woman. After cleaning the house top to bottom and checking her phone at least a dozen times, she found herself becoming angry. Why the hell wasn't he responding? What had she done? From her perspective she had never done anything but be honest with him.

As she rinsed out a mug she found under Finn's bed, it suddenly hit her. Maybe he wasn't answering because he didn't want to tell her he was dating someone else, and he figured this was a simple way to handle it. Could that be it? She ignored how her stomach hurt at the thought of him with another woman. It was one thing to just be friends because that was the way she wanted it, but if he became interested in someone else…

No, that couldn't be it. He would have told her. She thought of the things she tried to teach the boys.

If you wanted to know something, just ask, rather than dance around it. She pulled her phone out.

Hi, it's me again. What's going on? Before the night Finn got hurt, we texted each other all the time. I've been texting you, but you either aren't answering at all or your answers are wicked short. Did I do something wrong?

An hour later, Dot looked at her phone in disbelief. It seemed Boone couldn't be bothered to answer, even after her blunt question. She picked up her purse with a sigh, deciding she would run to the store for a few things, make herself dinner, and wait for the boys to get dropped off after hockey.

Twenty minutes later, she paused at the edge of the store parking lot. If she turned left, she would be going home. If she chose to turn right, she would be going by Boone's house. Should she see if he was home? If there was another car there, did it mean he had a date? This was stupid; it was time to go home and act like an adult. If they were just friends, she should be okay with whatever was going on and be able to just wait for a response.

The next thing Dot knew, she was turning her right blinker on and heading away from her house. Fuck being a reasonable adult. She wanted to see what was going on, that's all.

As she drove, she talked out loud without even realizing it. "I'm not going to stop by, this is just a drive-by. If the house is dark and no one seems to be there, then maybe he's at work or something, and that's why he didn't reply."

As she crested the hill by Boone's house, Dot could see lights blazing in the house, no extra cars. She took the sharp turn into his driveway, spraying a few pieces of gravel as she went. He was home alone, and he couldn't respond?

She pulled to a quick stop, threw the car in park, and jumped out. She stomped to the front door and raised her hand to knock just as the door opened.

By the look on his face, she knew she had caught him by complete surprise. "Dot," he exclaimed.

"What the fuck is your problem?"

His eyes widened. "Well, hi to you too."

"What's wrong with you?" she demanded.

"Jesus, Dot, it's cold out here. At least come inside if you're going to yell at me."

"I'm not yelling!" she shouted. She stepped into the front hallway, nearly slamming the door behind her.

He grinned. "Really?"

It took a sizable effort, but she tried to calm her anger. What the hell was wrong with her? She never got angry like this. "Fine. I won't yell."

"Thank you."

She looked up at him, suddenly feeling very unsure of herself. "Boone, what's happening? You don't answer my texts, and when you do, you answers are like you don't want to hear from me. Did I do something wrong?"

Dot watched as Boone tensed. "I answered your text. You asked about my week, and I responded."

"I've sent you several since then, and you didn't respond at all," she exclaimed.

His shoulders drooped, as if in defeat. "My phone has been off since I texted you."

"Why? Your phone is never off."

Boone looked up at the ceiling, knowing he had to tell her the truth. Shit! "Because I can't do this anymore. I thought I could, but I can't."

She gave him a quizzical look. "Can't do what?"

He gazed at her beautiful face, noting the flush of her cheeks from her earlier upset. Oh, how he wanted to reach out and just touch her face. "The buddies thing isn't working for me."

Cold fear washed over her. "What do you mean?"

"When I asked you out, and you said no, but we could be friends, I thought I was okay with that."

"Me too. I've loved our time together."

He extended a gentle hand to stroke her cheek. "But the other night, when Finn got hurt, everything changed."

"What do you mean, because of the boys?" For a split second, her anger began to bubble up again.

"No." He grinned. "I love the boys. This has to do with you and me, period."

"Then I don't understand the problem."

"You remember when you hugged me in the kitchen that night?"

"Yes."

"And then you kissed my cheek."

"Yes."

"Then, you kissed me goodnight when you tucked the boys in."

"Yes," she whispered.

"I was awake most of that night."

Without thinking, she whispered, "So was I."

His eyes were dark with emotion. "And the thing is, I was awake because I came to a hard realization." He looked down at his feet. "I realized that I want you. I want to be in your life. And not just as a friend, but as the man you are dating, the man who gets to hold your hand while watching a movie."

"Oh."

"I know it would be tricky with the boys, I know it would be a shift for your life. I know all of that. But I also know I didn't want to put you in an awkward position by talking about it, so I thought it best if I sort of faded away."

"Oh."

"I'm sorry, Dot. I should have told you the truth that day. I left before you got up because the thought of having coffee with you seemed so intimate. I knew I couldn't do it without wanting to kiss you."

"Oh."

Her brain was racing, and she could feel her heart doing the same. He was going to walk out of her life. She had always eagerly anticipated their Friday evenings together. She even put makeup on before he came over, something she had rarely done in recent years. And now Boone was walking away because she declined his offer to go out, citing the fact that she was not interested while her boys were still young. Her personal vow was going to force him out of her life.

"Look," said Boone, "I know this is awkward; I get it. I'm sorry for that, and now that you know, I'm sure you want to get out of here. 'Night, Dot." Boone turned away and started toward the kitchen.

"Boone."

He stopped but did not turn around.

"Please look at me." Without saying another word, she launched herself at him. She reached up, cupped his face in her hands, and kissed him, full on the lips.

Dot felt heat swamp her as Boone wrapped his arms around her. She pressed her body to his as she kissed him, and almost groaned in pleasure as his body responded instantly.

Embarrassment swept over her as she pulled back. She could feel the heat of her cheeks, and knew she was blushing like an idiot. "I am so sorry."

Boone tried to understand what was happening, "You're sorry? For what?"

"For kissing you like that."

Was it shock on his face? Boone lowered his arms and took a small step back from her. "You're sorry you kissed me?" He took another step back. "Maybe you should just leave."

"I'm not sorry we kissed," she said. "I'm sorry I jumped you like that." She sounded irritated and she looked quite unsure, suddenly seeming younger than her years. "Boone, listen to me. When you didn't text me back, I was convinced you were seeing someone else, and it really bothered me." She smiled slowly. "But now I've changed my mind." She reached out, and without speaking, he took her hand. "Ask me out again," she said. "Please."

He grinned. "Dot, will you go out with me?" His grin widened. "On a date?"

"Yes."

He took her other hand, pulled her close, and leaned down to gently kiss her. "Thank you," he chuckled. "Took you long enough to say yes."

Just then her stomach growled, loudly. He tipped his head. "Have you had dinner?"

"No."

"When do the boys get home?"

"Between eight and nine."

He checked his watch. "Well, date of mine," he grinned, "come eat dinner with me. I made more than enough, and it can be our first date."

After helping her off with her coat, Boone led Dot to the kitchen and pointed to one of the counter stools. "Have a seat and keep me company while I finish up. Do you want a glass of wine?"

"Please."

She watched in fascination as he walked around the kitchen, snagging two wine glasses from the hanging rack and an open bottle of merlot. He put them all on the counter and poured them each a glass. She grinned, realizing she had told this beautiful, sexy man that she would go out with him. This amazing man wanted her. Holy crap, it was almost mind-blowing. She crooked her finger, "Come here."

"As you wish." His eyes were warm as he walked around the counter.

Once he was next to her, she pulled him down to her and kissed him.

He gave a sexy growl before reciprocating. She could sense how hard he was working to keep his response in check, and she appreciated it. After all, it had been almost eight years since she had kissed a man.

When she pulled back, she was breathless, and for the first time in many years, she felt like a desirable woman. Wow, that was nice. She was still flustered when she smiled up at Boone.

He stroked her cheek. "I don't know what changed your mind, but damn, I'm glad."

"Me too."

He handed her a glass of wine before sitting down with her. With a sexy smile, he raised his glass. "To our first date."

Giggles threatened to swamp her. "To our first date."

For the next few minutes, the conversation stayed light. Boone got up and returned with two bowls of stew and a loaf of French bread.

"That smells really good," said Dot. "What is it?"

"Moroccan stew."

She took a spoonful and blew on it, then took a bite. She smiled. "This is amazing."

"Thank you." He took a bite, then put his spoon down to take a sip of wine. His eyes were dark and warm as he studied her. "So, what the heck happened?"

She knew what he was asking, and she brushed aside her inclination to squirm. Instead, she straightened her posture, took a sip of wine, then looked him straight in the eye.

"The morning after Finn's accident, when I woke up to the smell of coffee, all I could think about was how much I wanted to simply sit and enjoy your company over a warm mug. I tried to think of us as just friends, but I waited all week for you to text me, stop by, or something. Every time I sent you a text, I either got a very brief reply, or no response at all." She took another sip of her wine, hoping to invoke some liquid courage as she continued. "Then I had myself convinced you were seeing someone, and that really bothered me. So, if I'm being totally honest, I drove by tonight to see if there was another car here." Her nerves prompted her to titter. "When I came over the hill and found no one else to be here, I was so mad at you for not responding that I stormed in here like a crazy woman."

"Yeah, you might say that." He grinned. "You were clearly pissed."

"I was." She twirled the stem of the glass in her fingers, then looked at him. Her expression grew serious. "Boone, I don't know how to do this."

"Do what?"

"Date someone." She looked down and stirred the stew to buy the time she needed to express herself. "I was sixteen the last time I dated, and I ended up marrying him, so I have no idea how this works as an adult."

Boone reached out to twine his fingers through hers. "Hey, this is just as weird for me. I may have dated a bit more than you, but I've never dated a mom." He squeezed her hand. "We'll figure it out as we go, okay?"

Her eyes twinkled. "Okay," she said, "after all, I stormed in here and made an ass of myself, so things can only get easier now, right?"

"Right," Boone laughed.

Part-way through dinner, Dot silently gazed across the counter at him. Boone finally picked up his wine glass, took a sip, and said, "Yes? Ask whatever it is…"

"How do you know I want to ask anything?"

"It's written all over your face." He laughed. "I wouldn't suggest a career in poker, by the way."

"Fine," she said, patting her mouth with her napkin, then resting her arms on the counter. "I kissed you, and yet I don't even know if Boone is your first or last name."

"Last."

"Seriously?" She shook her head. "That's all you're going to tell me?"

He grinned like a kid. "You didn't ask anything else, sweetheart. I answered your question."

"Boone!"

He reached out to stroke her hand. "Sebastian Boone. No one, other than my great-aunt Stella and my abuela calls me Sebastian."

"Sebastian…" She nodded. "I like it." She stopped, catching something he had said. "Your abuela?"

"Yeah." He pointed to a small, framed portrait on the corner hutch. "My mom and I lived with my grandparents when I was a kid."

"Oh." Should she ask? She should. "No dad?"

"No." His eyes were serious. "I don't know who my dad is, but I had a great mom, and a great extended family."

"Hispanic."

"Mexican-American. My grandparents came to the U.S. when they were young, before my mom and her siblings were born."

"And where are they now?"

"My mom was killed in a car accident five years ago, shortly after my grandfather died. My grandmother died last year."

"I am so sorry."

"Me too."

It was time to talk about something other than death. "And, by the way, what the hell are you and PJ doing now that you've left the military?"

"We really didn't fully leave; we are still contracted to teach a bit, but we started our own corporate security firm."

"What does that mean?" Dot scooped up a spoonful of the stew, awaiting his answer.

"It means that companies, like Eismann, hire us to make sure that both their properties, like the factory, are protected. We hire security, set up their surveillance systems, run background checks on their potential hires, things like that."

"Oh."

"We also oversee electronic protection, meaning internet security."

Dot was impressed. "You do all of that?"

He shook his head. "No, I don't. But PJ and I organize, facilitate, and monitor it all."

"Wow." Emboldened, she continued. "And what sort of schedule does all of that translate to?"

The look he gave her was one of pure carnal desire, and Dot felt a glorious rush of heat. "It means I make my own schedule," he said. "It means that when you have the time to be with me, I can make that happen. There are benefits to being the boss."

"Oh."

Boone poured more wine into their glasses. "My turn. What is Dot short for? Dorothy?"

"No, but don't I wish."

"What do you mean?"

"Everyone assumes it's short for Dorothy, and it's not. It's short for Theodora."

"Theodora." He paused. "Theodora." Before Dot could say anything, he smiled. "I like it."

"I don't. But that's neither here nor there."

"Okay. And you're still working at the school, putting up with Georgie?"

She nodded. "I am. But now that she's announced she's leaving at the end of the school year, I don't really know what will happen. I think Angus will move up to principal, but that isn't official yet."

Boone felt a rush of jealousy. "Angus, the guy who asked you out?"

"How do you know that?"

Boone shrugged. "Shit, okay, you'll probably be mad, but Georgie told me."

She grinned. "And how did you feel about that?"

"I wanted to hit him," he said with a laugh. "Happy?"

"Yes," she said, giving him a smirk.

"Do you like working there?"

"I like working for, or with, Georgiana. But as for the job itself, I would be perfectly happy to do something else."

"Like what?"

Dot felt herself blush. She didn't talk with anyone about this. "Paint. I wish I could paint full time."

"You should. You certainly have the talent."

"Thank you." She averted her eyes, nervous. "I actually applied for a grant."

"What do you mean?"

"I haven't told anyone, but I applied for a grant that would pay me to paint for a year."

"Wow. When will you know if you got it?"

"A couple of months." Her smile grew. "I checked their website yesterday, and I'm still in the running. So, maybe…"

"That would be amazing."

"It would."

Chapter Fourteen

Boone chuckled as Dot began gathering the dinner dishes. "Leave it all there," he said. "I'll take care of everything later."

She shook her head. "Let's do it together."

"What, you can't stand the thought of a night without doing the dishes?"

She shook her head. "No, I just don't want our first date to make work for you."

They cleaned in companionable silence and the kitchen was gleaming just minutes later. Dot looked at her watch and sighed. "I need to head home soon, the boys will be dropped off before long."

Leaning against the counter, Boone looked at Dot, and she felt powerful and beautiful, seeing the look in his eyes

She had said yes, and she had kissed him. She felt like the whole world was opening anew.

He spoke, "I can go with you, or not. It's up to you."

Dot walked toward him slowly, enjoying the look in his eyes. It had been too long since a man had looked at her in such a way. She knew she was a different woman now than she was back then. She reached out to link her hands behind his neck and stretched up to kiss him. Hmm... She could get used to kissing a man who towered over her. Mike had been tall, but not like Boone. Somehow, standing like this with him made her feel delicate and protected. With a happy sigh, she stepped back. "I need to talk to the boys tonight, to tell that we are going to go out together, so I need to do this alone."

He nodded. "I understand."

She stroked his cheek. "I'll call you later, after they go to bed."

"Good."

Taking his hand, she smiled. "Now walk me to the door and kiss me goodbye?"

He snagged her coat from the foyer and helped her into it. "Nah, I'm walking you to the car and kissing you there."

"An even better idea."

At the car, Dot looked up at him, her eyes sparkling in the floodlights. "I'll talk to you in a bit," she said.

"I know." He pulled her hand up to his lips and kissed it. "Thank you."

"For what?"

"For giving this a chance."

She leaned against his broad chest. "You are welcome, and thanks for not kicking me out tonight."

She hugged him tightly. "I'm a little scared, but I can't walk away from you," she whispered.

"We'll figure it out." He kissed her hair. "One more kiss, then you need to go. We don't want your kiddos getting home to an empty house."

The boys wolfed down their frozen pizza while Dot listened to their tales from the day. When they were done, she said, "Guys, I need to talk to you about something."

Declan nodded. "Sure, Mom. What?"

Dot looked down at her hands and folded them on the table. "I was thinking I'd like to start dating Boone. What do you think?"

Finn turned to his brother, clearly confused. "We kind of thought you were already dating, Mom. I mean, except for last week, he's been here every Friday night since he moved here."

Declan shrugged. "And you put makeup on before he comes over. You never do that unless you're going to work or to one of our school events."

Dot laughed. "So, you guys assumed we were already a couple?"

They both nodded, and chorused, "Yes."

After the boys had gone to bed, Dot took a cup of herbal tea to her rocking chair in the living room and dialed Boone's number. "Hey."

"Hey. How'd it go?"

Dot chuckled. "They thought we were already an item. They looked at me like I had ten heads. It was almost too easy, but they clearly have no issue with it."

"Feel better?"

"I do, I'm glad I told them. Since they are more astute than I gave them credit for, it wasn't a big deal to them. They even pointed out that I've been putting makeup on when you come over."

"You don't need makeup, sweetheart. You in your fixing-the-garage-door outfit makes me as crazy as you all dressed up. But I'm glad it went well."

"Me too."

After their phone call, Dot decided a bubble bath was the perfect ending to this notably odd and emotional day.

As the tub filled, she undressed and stood in front of the full-length mirror. Her hair was short and fluffy, no longer the flame red of her childhood, but more of a lustrous auburn. Her eyes were an interesting mélange of green and blue that changed with the light, and freckles dusted her nose and cheekbones. Even after giving birth to the two boys and nursing them, her breasts were high and firm, and her waist was just as small as it had been when she was a newlywed. It had been a long time since Dot thought of herself as a desirable woman, a sexual being. Her needs had been taken care of by battery-operated stand-ins for a long time. But now? The hottest man she had ever seen wanted to date her.

Dot was not naïve. She could feel the intensity of his desire for her when they kissed. A giggle welled up inside her as she could feel the impressive, rock-hard package pressed against her. Damn, just thinking about it made her feel lightheaded. Boone wanted her. He liked *her*. And they were dating, whatever that meant.

Dot slid into the hot water and sighed contentedly. Life was suddenly becoming more exciting.

Chapter Fifteen

"It isn't like that," Boone said as he shook his head at PJ. "It isn't like that at all."

PJ really wanted to understand. "Then what is it like?"

"Remember back to high school, maybe the first girl you dated?"

"Yeah, so? You're a grown man, dating a grown woman. Beyond being grown, she's been married, so it's not like she's never dated."

"I know, but in some ways, it's like that."

"What the hell are you talking about?"

"Look, she married her high school sweetheart. That was her *only* dating experience. So, it's basically like that first girl you dated, trying to figure out how fast or slow to go. Add in two kids, jobs, and her wrestling with her grief and guilt about dating anyone, and it's moving pretty slowly. From a physical perspective, anyway."

"Is that a problem?"

"No, it's not a problem." He paused. "It'll work out."

"And the boys?"

"What about them?"

"Do you really want a full-blown instant family?"

"That's not the issue right now. I'm more concerned with the fact that she goes a bit overboard with the boys, making sure they don't feel neglected."

"And that's a problem?"

"Look, I really like those kids, but I want Dot, and once in a while I want to be the center of the fucking universe, okay?"

It all sounded like a lot to PJ. "Is she worth it?"

"Oh, hell, yes."

Boone thought about that conversation as he drove to Dot's house, the aroma of the pizza in the passenger seat making his stomach growl. He pulled into the driveway and parked in front of the garage.

By the time he reached the door, Dot was waiting for him. "Here, let me take those," she said, relieving him of the pizzas.

She took the boxes to the kitchen table, then turned to look at him. The look in her eyes drove all doubt from Boone's heart and mind. She was definitely as into him as he was her. "Hi," she said.

"Hi." He placed his hands on her shoulders and leaned down to kiss her.

Starting slowly, the kiss quickly deepened. God only knew how far it would have gone if Finn hadn't yelled from the next room. "Mom, is Boone here?"

Dot pulled back and sighed. "Grrr."

Boone laughed. "Yup."

"Yes, Finn." She took his hand in hers, then called over her shoulder. "Wash up for dinner, boys."

The pizza was long gone, the movie watched. Dot stirred beside Boone, where she was curled up against him, his arm around her. "Time for bed, guys."

The normal grumbling ensued. It wouldn't be a night in their house without at least one of the two boys griping about having to go to bed. Dot rolled her eyes as she stood up, quickly dropping a kiss on Boone's cheek. "I'll be back in a few."

"Sounds good."

The boys yelled their goodnights down to Boone, then the house went quiet as he waited for Dot to return. She walked into the living room and dimmed the overhead lights. "Wine?"

Dot returned minutes later with a bottle of wine in one hand, two glasses in the other. "You can pour," she said.

Boone followed her lead and handed her a glass. "Cheers."

"Cheers." Dot took a sip, something clearly on her mind.

Boone stroked her hand where it sat on his thigh. "You okay?"

Her answer was quick. "I am." She put her glass down on the coffee table. "I want to ask you something."

She sounded so serious, he suddenly felt worried. "Okay." He wondered what was going on.

"And if it doesn't interest you, I need you to be honest, okay? Promise?"

What the hell was she about to say? "I promise."

Dot stood up and walked quickly to the window, her back to him. "I'm going to Burlington next weekend. The boys are going to a hockey clinic, and we always stay over in a hotel for the Saturday night."

"Okay." Was she asking him to stay with them all in one room? He could do that; he would just have to mask his desire for her when they were in front of the boys. Anything for more time with her...

"And this year, the boys have been invited to go with friends. Davy and Jamison, you know, the twins they hang out with all the time?"

"Yes."

"So, I already have the hotel room booked, and I was wondering if you'd like to go with me." She stammered. "I have to have them there for seven in the morning, but you could drive over with us, or meet me there. We could get dinner, walk around, then..."

Boone padded across the room in his sock feet. He wrapped his arms around her from behind, feeling the tension in her body. Well, this certainly dealt with his concern about taking it slow with this fascinating and sexy woman; she was inviting him into her bed. He rubbed her arms, pulling her into his warmth. "I would love to join you," he said.

Her body relaxed immediately. "You would?"

He kissed her just below the ear, taking a moment to breathe in her scent. God, she always smelled so incredibly good. His voice was husky. "Dot, babe, I want to be with you all the time. I'm doing everything I can to respect your situation, and I don't want to put too much pressure on you, but I want you more than I can say. I would love to go up north with you."

Turning in his arms, Dot reached up and pulled him down to kiss her. As soon as their lips touched, Boone knew something had shifted. She was ready to be with him. *With* him. Shit! How did he get so lucky to be with such an amazing woman?

He pulled back, knowing he was reaching a point where he was going to press the issue right here and now. "Come, sit with me and have some wine. Then we can plan out what we want to do in Burlington." Dot pursed her lips. Boone raised an eyebrow. "What? What's that look for?"

She giggled. "I was going to say that all I want to do in Burlington is go to bed with you."

He tugged her hand, leading her to the couch. "Watch it, lady, or I may just throw you over my shoulder right now and take you to bed."

Chapter Sixteen

"Jesus, man. Your head is so far gone today, you might as well have stayed home," PJ groused, leaning back in his office chair.

Boone was on the other side of the desk, his feet up on PJ's desk, knowing how much it irritated his friend. "Fuck off, man. My head is just fine today. I'm looking forward to my weekend."

"Fine," PJ laughed as he looked at his watch, "it's after five o'clock. Go grab us two cold ones."

Boone did just that, returning with two frosty bottles of beer. Their assistant clocked out by four on Fridays, so it was just the two of them in their new office suite. So far, business had been so good, they already needed to hire three additional guards to fulfill their security contracts. Maybe someday they would miss the excitement of the SEALs, but for now, having a regular schedule, warm beds, and guaranteed safety was a welcome change. "Cheers."

"*Salud*, man." PJ took a swig. "So, are you riding with them to Burlington, or driving up there yourself?"

"Driving myself."

"Are you going to her house for dinner tonight?"

"No. She's getting the boys organized for the weekend, and I think she wanted to make them feel like she wasn't abandoning them by not staying in the same hotel."

"I bet they're thrilled to have just some guy time."

"Yeah, I think so. Anyway, she suggested we take one car, but I know she isn't ready for the boys to know we're having sex, so I said I'd meet her there. We can't check in until noon anyway. Besides, she's getting on the road around six a.m., so I thought I'd run over to her place after she leaves and paint the kitchen. She's had the paint for over a month but hasn't had the time to do it. I thought I could surprise her. It's a small kitchen and it's a pretty simple paint job, so I should be able to knock it out in a few hours if I focus."

"Painting her kitchen…" PJ's expression was serious. "You really like her, huh?"

Boone nodded. "I do." He looked down at the bottle in his hands. "Shit, PJ. I didn't plan this, you know? I mean, I've always thought she was cute, then it was a challenge to see if she'd warm up to me that way. But before I knew it, I realized I really like being around her. And now she's all I think about. I can't wait to see her, to talk to her, to even get a text from her."

"Jesus, you sound like a girl."

"I know! Shit, I'm like a fucking pre-teen when it comes to her. I'm about five seconds away from writing notes with little hearts on them."

PJ snorted, trying to hold in his laughter. Boone rolled his eyes. "Go ahead and laugh, I know it's funny."

"I tried, man, I'm really trying not to laugh, but you're killing me with this shit. I swear to God, if any of the guys hear this, you are never, ever going to stop getting shit, you know that, right?"

"I do."

"And the boys? Are you ready for that?"

"I don't know," Boone said. "Right now, it's awesome. They see me as someone cool. If this seems to really go somewhere, I don't know how that will go. They've had her undivided attention for most of their lives, at least the part they remember."

"You know that if this works out, you assume instant parenthood, right? Instant *father*hood, to be precise."

"I know."

"Let's face it, neither one of us had a father growing up."

Boone took a swig. "True, but we did have great male role models. You had your grandfather and Shroom, and I had my abuelo."

"True." PJ nodded. "I still miss your abuelo. He was one hell of a man."

"He was. We both got lucky with our grandparents."

PJ leaned back and placed his feet on the desk too, which was almost unheard of for him. "What about the memory of her husband? How does that play into all of this?"

"His picture is there, all over the place. It's even on the bedside table."

"Since when have you been in her bedroom?"

Boone scoffed. "That was months ago. She was showing me her paintings, that's all. But, yeah, if we get together, I may need to take a stance on Mike staring at me when we go to bed. Shit, it would be like he was there to critique my performance."

PJ tried to keep a straight face. Laughing, he replied, "You might want to work on how you word that thought when you express it to Dot."

The next day, Boone drove into the hotel parking lot. He had painted Dot's kitchen, cleaned up, and returned everything to its place, even adding a bouquet of flowers to the table. He couldn't wait for her to see how good it all looked.

Before he got out of the truck, he texted her.

Hi - want some company?

Hell, yes! Room 305.

In the lobby, he followed the signs to the guestrooms then strode to the stairwell. An elevator would only take longer.

At Room 305, he took a deep breath, then knocked. He laughed at the sound of Dot's voice through the door. "Who is it?"

"Room service, ma'am."

She opened the door, stepping aside to let him in. "You better have that roast beef sandwich I ordered."

Boone dropped his overnight bag, then turned and picked her up in his arms so he could kiss her deeply. He smiled as she wrapped her legs around him. Damn, he wanted this woman. Still holding her, he pulled back a bit. "No sandwich, only me. What shall we do instead of eating lunch?"

Dot grinned mischievously. "How about we go get lunch, then stay in for the rest of the day?"

And that was what they did. After a nice lunch at a pub, they stopped at Trader Joe's for some wine and snacks, took a long walk along the waterfront, and headed back to the room. By late afternoon, Finn and Declan had called to tell them all about their hockey workshop and the exciting plans they had for dinner and indoor swimming at their hotel.

The call over, Dot turned to Boone. "I'm going to take a shower, so how about a glass of wine when I'm done? We could look at the lake."

"I'll open the cabernet," he said.

Boone organized the wine and two chairs so they could look out over the water. He could hear her showering and had to fight his body's reaction to the idea of her naked body under that hot water. He had never waited this long to be intimate with a woman and he had been dreaming of how she would taste and feel.

Still staring out at the dark water below, Boone realized Dot had come to stand behind him. Turning, he felt like a sledgehammer had hit him in the chest. Dot stood before him, clad in a soft silky top that left little to his already overactive imagination, and matching shorts that showed off her perfect legs. "Jesus, you are beautiful."

"Thank you." She was blushing. "I know I'm not…"

"Not what?" He reached out to stroke her cheek, not trusting himself to touch her body yet. He didn't want to spook her.

"I'm not perfect like George, I know that," she whispered.

Boone's eyes widened in disbelief. "Dot, you are gorgeous." He pulled her toward him, sensing she needed to be held. "You… *You* are the woman I want. Body and soul. Not anyone else. *You.* You turn me on so much, I've been going crazy for months, trying to keep my hands off you. The thought of you keeps me awake at night, and you haunt my dreams." He leaned down to kiss the side of her neck, hungrily taking in her scent again. "You, no one else."

"Oh." Dot leaned against him. "Thank you."

"For what? I haven't done anything yet."

That struck her as funny, and she started to laugh. "Go take your shower, soldier. I need you to keep me warm if I'm going to wear this outfit, got it?"

His eyes widened as he watched her nipples press against the thin fabric. "I promise to make you hot, sweetheart."

They sat together in the large armchair, drinking, nibbling on the charcuterie board they had prepared together, and talking. Each sip of wine seemed to bring them closer to heading to the wide bed behind them, as their hands roamed, and their kisses became longer and hotter.

Dot climbed off his lap, giggling as she wobbled. "I think I'm tipsy."

Boone stood quickly. "Then by all means, let me help you to bed."

Slowly, he reached out to slide his hand up under the hem of her shirt, and Dot held in a groan, wanting him so badly, it was all he could do to keep from tearing both of their clothes off.

The last button now undone, Dot pushed the shirt off his shoulders, then reached down to peel off her own top, tossing it to the side. She leaned forward and pressed her breasts against his chest.

Boone pressed her back onto the cool sheets. "I need to look at you, babe. I have waited so long for this. I need to see you." He stroked one fingertip from the rapid pulse in her neck down toward the shadow between her breasts. There were two tiny heart tattoos on her left breast, and he stroked them reverently. "What do they symbolize?"

"The boys."

"Damn lucky artist."

She smiled, then reached out to trace the symbol on his upper arm. "And this?"

"My SEAL unit."

Conversation stopped then, as they kissed and explored each other. Finally, Boone slipped out of his pants and reached for the waistband of her shorts, sliding them down her legs. He kissed her. "I want to taste you, are you okay with that?"

"God, yes."

Boone moved so he could brace himself, then leaned down to kiss just above her auburn curls. Slowly, he touched the tip of his tongue to the edge of her lips there and she moaned and nearly bucked him off the bed. She was so ready for him, and he was dying to bury himself in her.

He continued to taste her, savoring her smell and her sweetness, until he knew he needed more. Later, he would fully pleasure her this way, but now he needed to join with her.

As he moved over her, he looked down, amazed anew at the power of emotion and desire he felt for this woman.

Keeping his desire in check as much as he could, he moved in such a way that the head of his manhood lightly pressed against her, waiting for signs that she was ready too. She reached up, cradling his face in her hands, and kissed him.

The kiss did not feel right. Boone pulled back to look down at her and saw pain in her eyes. "Dot, what's wrong?"

"Nothing." She smiled, but the smile didn't reach her eyes. "Let's…"

Boone rolled off her and pulled her into his arms. He felt the tension in her body. "What's going on?"

"Nothing." She buried her face in his chest. "I just…"

"What?" He kissed her temple. "Tell me."

"You might get mad."

"No, I won't. What's going on?"

A drop fell to his chest, and Boone realized Dot had started to cry. "Shh, baby, it's okay. Whatever it is, it's okay."

"I can't do this. I feel too guilty. I married Mike, and now…" Her voice sounded so sad it made his heart hurt.

He finished the sentence. "And now you were about to have sex with me."

"Yes. And I don't think I can do it." She started to sit up. "I'll go, Boone. I'll go. I'm so sorry."

He pulled her close again. "You're not going anywhere. You can stay right here with me, no strings attached, okay?"

"You mean it?" Her voice shook. "You don't deserve this. I am so sorry."

He gently stroked her back, willing his touch to convey a gentle safety without the sexual overtones.

"You have nothing to be sorry for, sweetheart. Just sleep. It's okay."

"Really?"

"Really."

Chapter Seventeen

Dot fell asleep with her head on Boone's chest. As she slept, Boone stared up at the ceiling. What the hell was happening? How had they gone from her emerging from the bathroom in that sexy little number to her being moved to tears at the idea of being intimate with him?

Could this be fixed? Could it change? What would it take for her to be ready for this important step in their relationship? She stirred in her sleep, and he pulled her closer, kissing her forehead. He loved her. The realization hit him hard. He loved her. He was head over heels in love with her.

Shit, how had *that* happened? Boone felt a surge of something damn close to panic fill him. *In love*. He hadn't thought he was in love for more than a decade. He dated, he'd had lovers, he loved Georgiana, but he hadn't been *in love* with anyone for a hell of a long time. And now he was in love with Dot? There was no doubt she was amazing; she was the real deal, the full package. She was smart, sexy, funny, passionate, opinionated, strong, and loyal. On her own, she would have made any man stupid with love. But she was also a widow who couldn't seem to move past the death of her husband, and she came with two pre-teen boys. And Atticus. Boone smiled. He hadn't had a dog since he was a kid, and he had to admit, Atticus rocked. He loved how the dog followed him around, ears touching the ground much of the time, looking for a treat or a snuggle.

Boone was in love with a woman who came with a whole tractor trailer full of emotional baggage and complications. And he didn't know how she felt about him. He also didn't know if she would ever make love with him. Could he be celibate if it meant being with her in every other way?

Was she with him emotionally or not? It seemed like she wanted to be, but Mike still lurked in the shadows. Would it ever just be the two of them, without him between them?

Boone shook his head, then looked down at Dot as she slept. It was time to stop trying to plan out his life. He was snuggled up with the woman he loved; he needed to enjoy this moment and let what was meant to happen, happen.

With a yawn, he carefully moved under the comforter, kissing her temple one more time before he closed his eyes.

Dot awoke and immediately recalled where she was. She was in a king-sized bed in the hotel, held protectively in Boone's arms, and covered only by one of his shirts.

Shame washed over her, and she felt tears threaten to prickle her eyes again. How could she have treated him that way? Her grandmother would have called her a tease in the nastiest of tones. And she was right. She had bought a sexy outfit, invited him to spend the night with her, and then gotten naked with him.

And then she froze. Just before he entered her, something she had fantasized about for a while, guilt hit. It felt like she was cheating on Mike. Was she? Was it wrong to be with Boone? What would Mike want her to do?

Dot thought back to her husband; the way they had loved each other, and still did. The love between them had not died just because his physical body had perished. There were times she still felt his presence and his influence. Would he really want her to remain alone for the rest of her life? She smiled as she remembered a conversation years before, about a year before Mike was killed, when he had commented about how sexy she was and how much "work" it was to keep her sexually satisfied. The conversation had made them both laugh, and he had often joked about doing his matrimonial duty in order to keep her happy.

For almost eight years, Dot had stayed true, aside from that pitiful night in Montreal. She would always honor his memory and keep it alive for herself and the boys, but maybe it was also time for her to live again. She was still in her early thirties, and she liked to think Mike would not expect her to be alone forever.

No, he wouldn't want that, she was sure of it. No one loved life and living it to the fullest more than Mike. A wave of emotion hit her, and she realized the absolute last thing Mike would want was for her to stop living, and yet she had done just that. She had done her best with the boys, that was true, but somewhere along the way she had also stopped living and growing for her own sake. As a woman.

She thought of all their dreams... The plan had been that Mike would renovate the old barn behind the house as a studio for her, and eventually, she would stop working at the school so she could devote her time to painting. That dream had died with Mike. Maybe it was time to inject new life into those dreams.

But first, it was time to decide about Boone. She shifted her body in order to get a better look at his face as he slept. His impossibly long lashes rested on his face. He was always tan, and until now she had attributed it to his years of southern living. Now that she knew of his heritage, she realized he was not just gloriously delicious to look at, but interesting too. The man was gorgeous with so many facets yet to explore. She already knew him to be funny (downright silly when warranted), intelligent, hardworking, understanding, and certainly resourceful and cool under pressure, as she had witnessed firsthand the night of the ice storm. Most importantly, he had not been pissed off when she hit the brakes on him tonight. He was a keeper. And yes, she wanted him. Desperately. It wasn't just that she hadn't had sex in years, it was that she wanted Boone.

Yes, it would be emotionally difficult to do this, she knew that. But it was time.

Boone awoke fully the second a soft, warm hand touched his manhood. What the fuck? Was it intentional, or was Dot just moving in her sleep? He needed to proceed with caution. The worst thing he could do was get so hard he started pressing against her. Shit, he was about to embarrass himself. Maybe he should have left after she pulled back.

The hand moved and began to slowly stroke him. *Whaat?* Boone shifted ever so slightly and looked down into Dot's eyes. She slid over so she was on top of him, and before he could do or say anything, she whispered, "Don't say a word. Not a word."

With that, she moved so his hard length was pressing against her soft, wet lips, and then, before he could fully understand what was happening, she moved to slide him deep inside her.

Her smile was serene as she found her rhythm. Slow and gentle at first, then faster and harder, until Boone knew he was close to his release. He held her hips and pulled her closer, hoping he could hold on long enough for her to reach her climax.

God, she felt so good. So tight and hot, and they fit together like they were meant for each other. Each time she moved against him, he tightened his grip on her, needing to be as deep inside her as possible.

Her tempo changed and she whispered his name reverently. As her body clasped his, he called out her name as he poured himself into her.

Chapter Eighteen

Dot lay on his chest, listening to his breathing as it slowed, his hand lightly tickling her lower back. "Am I allowed to say something now?"

She laughed in response to his playful tone. "Depends on what you're going to say. I reserve the right to tell you to stop talking."

"Did I miss something? I seem to remember being told you weren't ready, and then…"

Dot shrugged, still nestled in his arms. "I wasn't ready then." She braced herself, so she could look down at his face, lit ever so slightly by the streetlights outside. "I slept for a while, then woke up and got to thinking. I needed to get my head straight." She playfully nipped at his neck. "Then I decided there was no way I was letting you out of my bed without finally being with you."

"Ahh."

"What does 'ahh' mean?"

Almost effortlessly, he rolled them over, so he loomed over her. He leaned down and kissed her deeply, then said, "It means I am damn glad that you, as you put it, got your head straight. That's what it means."

"Me too."

He moved over her, and she could feel that he was ready again. Seeing the slow smile spread across her face, he dropped a kiss on her shoulder. "Does this mean I get to play now?"

"Hell, yes!"

By noon the next day, they had packed up and checked out of the hotel. Boone carried Dot's bag to her car and placed it in the trunk. "Okay, so in hindsight, we should have driven together."

She nodded. "Yup."

He grinned, supremely satisfied with himself. "I don't know, cupcake, you look tired. Some might think you didn't get a lot of sleep last night."

She pushed his back against the car, then stood on her tiptoes and linked her arms around his neck. They were eye to eye. "I barely got any sleep last night, *cupcake,* because there was this hottie with a hard-on in my bed, and he seemed to be insatiable."

He pulled her close. "He was, although I do remember who started things."

"Me too." She kissed him quickly. "I need to go. I'll call you tonight?"

"Great."

"Want to come for dinner tomorrow night?"

"I do." He stroked her cheek. "I am going to miss you tonight. We are going to need to talk about what we're doing, at some point."

"I'm going to miss you too." She bit her lower lip. "Maybe we could start with some alone time when the guys are off at practice?"

"You tell me when, and I'll be there, or you can come to my house."

He had just started cooking dinner when the phone rang. He smiled, seeing it was Dot. "Hello?"

"I can't believe you did this!" Her happiness was clear. "It is so beautiful, Boone, thank you. I can't tell you how much I appreciate it."

"I'm glad, baby. You kept saying you wanted to paint the kitchen, and I know how busy you are." His voice grew sincere, "Besides, you shouldn't waste your time painting a kitchen wall, you should be painting canvases. I can take care of the walls for you."

"That's the other thing I was calling to tell you."

"What?"

"I made it to the final round of the grant application process, Boone," she squealed. "It's down from two hundred artists to just five of us." She sounded like she could have popped.

"Holy, shit, baby, that is amazing!"

"I know!" She paused. "Anyway, I need to go, but I couldn't wait to tell you, and to thank you."

"Congrats, sweetie, and you're welcome, and I miss you."

"Me too. I'll call you later."

"Sounds good."

Three days later, Boone pulled into his driveway and parked his truck in the garage. Taking a quick look at his watch, he had about fifteen minutes before Dot was due to arrive. Just enough time to grab a quick shower.

When Dot opened the front door, Boone was sitting on the steps of the main staircase. "Hi."

She hung her coat on the rack. "Hi."

He stood and approached her slowly, almost catlike in his movements. "How was your day? How was work?"

"What work?" She grabbed his shirt and pulled him closer. "I have no idea what I did today, other than daydream."

He slid his hands up under the hem of her sweater and growled appreciatively as he brushed his hands along her warm skin. "And what were you daydreaming about, cupcake?"

"Home improvement. I was daydreaming about installing new flooring in my beautifully painted kitchen."

Boone had been pleased that she loved his paint job, but now he was enjoying her sense of humor. "Flooring, huh? Not daydreaming about the guy you could get to install it?"

She started unbuttoning his shirt. "Maybe that too. Know anyone?" she said playfully.

He took her hand and led her toward the stairs. "Come upstairs and let me see if I can surpass your daydreams."

They settled into a pattern. Three days a week, Dot raced to Boone's house when the boys were at hockey, wanting every possible moment with him. Other nights, Boone joined them for dinner at their house, or had them over to eat at his. Slowly, he started helping more around her house and with the boys, even taking them to practices when she had obligations at work.

One afternoon, Boone dropped the boys off at the rink, then drove back to Dot's. She wouldn't be home for at least another hour, so his plan was to put dinner in the oven, then go back for the boys.

He smiled at the sight of her car in the driveway. Her meeting must have ended early. He bounded up the steps. "Hi!"

Dot turned from the kitchen sink and smiled at him. "Hi."

"You're home early."

"The meeting got cancelled. I knew you already had the guys, so I thought I could get back here and start dinner." She licked her lips as she eyed him up and down. "But now that you're here, we could…"

They hadn't made love in her house yet, only his. Boone had not wanted to bring up the subject of

Mike's photos throughout the house, so he had been just fine with the arrangement. But now? His woman was gazing at him in a way his body immediately responded to. Jesus! He had never wanted a woman as much as he wanted Dot. "We could," he said.

She tossed the hand towel on the counter. "Follow me."

Boone followed her up the stairs, happy to watch her walk in front of him. Her curves were a gift, and he couldn't get enough of them. Touching them. Tasting them. Looking at them. She was spectacular, and she was his.

At the door to her bedroom, he took a deep breath to steel himself. Even if the picture was still there, he was determined to let it go and not say a word. No matter what, she was inviting him into her bed, in the room she had shared with Mike. He needed to honor that, and let the rest go.

Boone was shocked by what he saw next. The room was completely different from how he had remembered it. The furniture had been rearranged and the bed had been moved. The bedside stand had been replaced by a small bookcase and lamp, and the only picture there was one of Dot with the two boys. Dot stood at the end of the bed, gauging his reaction.

"Why didn't you tell me?" she said.

Boone was confused. "Tell you what?"

"How much it was bothering you."

"What are you talking about?"

Dot snorted. "Boone, you just walked up here, tension rolling off you in waves. No matter how much you want me, you were freaking out about being in this room, weren't you? Going to bed with me here, with the pictures of Mike still in the room?"

Boone stepped forward and pulled her into his arms. "I didn't tell you because I'm a dipshit. I didn't want to upset you, and I thought as long as we were together, I could pretend it didn't bother me."

"You are such a dipshit." She shook her head. "Boone, it's you and me now. I would never do that to you." She hugged him. "But I appreciate your protective nature."

"Always."

She pulled her blouse over her head in one smooth movement. Standing before him in only her skirt and bra, she grinned. "Get naked, *cupcake*. We don't have a lot of time, but damn it, I want all of you now."

Chapter Nineteen

Boone knew he was being an asshole, he really did. No matter how he tried to get his shit together, it wasn't working. He had barked at PJ all day, now he was yelling at Georgiana, and for the first time in their years of friendship, he realized he may have hurt her feelings when he snapped and said he didn't need to hear her voice right now. Fuck! This wasn't what he wanted to be doing, that was for sure.

He softened his approach. "Georgie, I'm sorry. I didn't mean that, I'm sorry. I'm being a dick, and you didn't deserve any of it."

Her eyes showed she was still upset, but she swallowed and gave him a wan smile. "What the hell is going on, Boone? What's wrong with you?"

His shoulders slumped. "Got time to talk?"

"Of course, I do. Come on in, and let's sit a while."

Georgiana pulled two beers from the fridge, then sat at the kitchen table and grinned at him. "We start trying to get pregnant next week, so my beer-drinking days are numbered."

He chuckled. "Well, thanks for taking the time to have one with me."

"My pleasure. Now, what the hell is going on to make you such a pain in the ass? PJ called today saying you seemed off, Jack noticed it yesterday, and you just bit my head off, too."

"I know." He took a swig. "Shit, even I hate me right now."

"No one hates you. Irritated by you, yes. But hate is a strong word. We all love you, but something is clearly going on."

"It is." He needed to talk to someone who might understand, or at least help him clear his head. "You know I've been seeing Dot," he began.

"Yeah, of course. I thought things were going so well."

"They are." He shrugged. "And they're not."

"What do you mean?"

"We have a great time together. We have dinner at least three or four times a week, we do things with the boys. On days the boys have practice, she stops by my house."

Georgiana tried to hide a grin. "To play Scrabble, you mean?"

"Of course." He wiggled his eyebrows. "I really like to play Scrabble with her."

"So, what's the problem?"

His voice rose. "The problem is, it's not going anywhere. Period. We are in the same rut now that we were in a month ago. Yes, the sex is fabulous. Yes, we have fun together. And I feel like a fucking boy toy."

Just then, Jack came into the kitchen. "Never thought I'd hear those words from you."

"Yeah, yeah."

Jack grinned at his friend. "This, I have got to hear." Retrieving a beer for himself, he joined them at the table. "Continue."

"Glad you came for the entertainment."

Jack chuckled. "Me too."

"Yes, assholes, I feel like a toy. I can be there for sex. I can fix the faucet. I can make dinner or drive the boys to practice. But spend the night at her house? No way. Ask the boys to do something like clear the table? Hell, no. And Declan is becoming a little prick, by the way." He looked at Georgiana. "Sorry for the language, Gi. But he's seriously been a pain in the ass."

"How so?" Georgiana knew both boys so well, she was surprised to hear this.

"Like last night, they came over for dinner. I grilled burgers, made fries in the air fryer. And Declan's only comment was that his dad wouldn't have made fries, he would have made tater tots. I mean, seriously. The guy has been dead since Dec was like maybe three years old or so. He probably doesn't even have memories of things like that. I don't know, maybe Dot tells them stories, but I really wish he didn't feel the need to bust my balls over such little shit like that."

"Ouch."

"Exactly. Then later, we were watching a movie, and Dec asked about the coffee table. I told him it was a gift from Parker when I moved to Vermont, and he scoffed. He made a point of telling me that all of the furniture in their house was made by his dad."

"Shit," said Jack.

"Yeah. And the thing is, when he does this shit, which is a lot now, Dot doesn't say or do anything. She just ignores him."

Georgiana reached out to pat his hand. "Aw, I'm sorry, Boone. Does she say anything later when Dec isn't there?"

"Not unless I bring it up. Then she says he's still getting used to me being around, and that I need to ignore him."

"Which makes it seem like your feelings don't matter."

Boone thought about that possibility. "I guess so, yeah. That's it. It's like I'm supposed to understand his feelings, and be the adult, which I get that I am, but when does she call him out on this shit? And will it change? Will we ever move past this stage?"

Georgiana shot a glance at Jack hearing the agitation in their friend's voice. "Boone, listen to me. I know it feels like this has been going on forever, but it hasn't. You are the first and only man that Dot has dated other than Mike. She's letting you into her world, into her bed. And yes, maybe she's letting Dec get away with things he shouldn't, but you can handle it if she really matters to you."

Boone's face grew grumpier with her words. Georgiana tipped her head. "Are you in love with her?"

"Why?"

"I'll take that as a yes."

"Yes, I'm in love with her, okay? Happy now?"

Georgiana pursed her lips, knowing a laugh would make things worse. "Yes, I am. Congratulations. Now stop being whiny. You need to man up and work through this."

Chapter Twenty

Boone stood in his kitchen, glaring at Dot. "Are you serious?"

Her hands were firmly planted on her hips. "I am."

"I'm asking you to go to Burlington with me for one night, so we can get away and have some alone time, and you're declining the invitation. I even made sure the boys had something great to do, and you're still shooting me down? What the fuck?"

"Don't raise your voice at me," she said, firmly holding her ground.

Boone was trying to control his temper, but it was hard. He had spent almost a week planning a romantic surprise, and it now was clearly not happening. "I'm not raising my voice. I'm asking you to explain."

"You can't make plans like that for me, Boone. That's not fair. How would the boys feel about me taking off that way?"

"How would the *boys* feel? The boys would be going with George and Jack, where they'd have a hell of a good time, be spoiled to death, and be safe. What about how I feel?"

"Boone! I appreciate your effort here, and I want to be with you, too, but you can't make plans for us off the cuff. I need to talk these things through with Dec and Finn before we decide something like this. What if they felt like I was ditching them?"

"How the holy hell could they feel that way? Your entire life, everything you do, revolves around them. It's not enough that you are the best parent they could possibly have, you go overboard. Shit, Dot, you made three different dinners last night so they would each have what they wanted. How is that real life? What happens when they can't always custom order what they want, when they want it?"

"Don't tell me how to raise my children! You know that's a hard limit for me," she exclaimed.

"I'm not telling you how to raise them. I'm trying to figure out how to make this work between us, and you're putting up roadblocks at every turn."

"How can you say that? I'm here now, aren't I?"

Boone felt sad as reality hit him. "Dot, here's the thing. I am in love with you." Her eyes widened. "I love you. But – and I hate putting a but in this conversation – I don't think you love me. If you do, you don't love me enough. Right now, I'm a fun diversion. Frankly, I feel like my primary purpose right now is to make you come, and as much fun as that is, and as much as I love you, I can't be just a diversion for you. If we are going to be together, part of that is for us to become a family, and you aren't letting that happen. You let Declan be a jerk, you let both of them walk all over you, and you don't let me have a say in anything. It's not working."

"What are you saying?"

"I'm saying that since your first reaction to hearing me say I love you is to look shocked, and that your next reaction was to ask me what I mean, I think we need to take a break. I'd like to say it's just a little break while we sort some things out, but it may be more than that. I can't fit the mold you seem to want to put me in, and I don't see any flexibility on your part to change the current situation."

He reached out to rest his hand on her cheek. "I love you too much to live like this."

Chapter Twenty-One

Days passed, then weeks. Dot rolled out of bed each morning, hoping there would be a text from Boone saying he was wrong, begging her to come back to him.

That text didn't arrive.

Some mornings, before the boys got up, she sat with her phone and thought about texting him. She drove home in shock that day he broke up with her. He was wrong; he was being a stubborn, selfish ass. She didn't need crap like that.

What was wrong with her putting her boys first? She babied them, so what? Yes, she had gone out of her way to make sure they didn't feel ignored when she had started dating Boone. Was that so wrong?

Of course, it wasn't wrong! She was a mother, first and foremost, and he could go fuck himself if he had an issue with that.

Sometimes, late at night, she thought back to the reason for the breakup. Was she wrong to have jumped down his throat when he'd been trying to do something romantic? No. Yes. Well, maybe not.

Could she have handled it better? Definitely. But if this was the way he was going to act, it was better that it had ended. After all, who proclaims their love during a fight, geez.

Fall arrived, and with it came the start of the hockey season again. Dot waffled between joy in watching the boys hit the rink, and the dread of the long hours she would devote to getting them to and from the practices and games, and the hours she would spend freezing at the rink. What the hell had Mike been thinking when he signed Dec up for Learn-to-Skate all those years ago? He'd always made such a big deal about wanting the boys to play hockey; she'd always felt she needed to do it for Mike. Now she had to keep it going.

The second night of the new season, Dot stopped short before turning into her usual parking spot. What the fuck? Boone's truck was already parked in the lot, two spaces down from where she planned to park.

She hadn't seen him in months. They had run into each other at the gas station, and they barely managed to say hello. Now he was at the rink? What was she going to do? Wait, why the hell was he at the rink? He had never gone there other than to shuttle the boys to and from practices.

Once the car was parked, she said, "Okay, grab your gear. Let's get you guys set to take the ice."

The boys raced up the ramp, happy to be skating again almost every day. Just then, Boone emerged from the tunnel and headed right for them.

Finn let out a shriek of joy. "Boone!"

Boone smiled at the younger boy. "Finn, good to see you!"

Finn rushed forward to give him a hug. "Are you playing?"

"I am, I joined the men's league." He smiled at Declan. "Hey, Dec."

Dec seemed happy to see him too. "Hey. What position?"

"Wing."

"Cool." Dec looked at his brother. "Come on, dorkus. Let's go, we need to get ready for practice. Bye, Boone."

"Bye, guys. Have a great practice."

Dot caught up just as the boys ran off. She found herself staring at Boone. He looked good. Better than good, fucking delectable. His hair was damp from the shower, his skin flushed from the exertion, and like always, his clothes fit him perfectly. One look at him, and she was ready to beg him to take her. Not take her back, that was far too complicated. But take her somewhere and work his magic.

Boone nodded at her. "Dot. How are you?"

"Fine. You?"

"Fine, thanks."

"Why are you here?"

"PJ, Jack, and I all signed up for the men's league."

"Oh, that's nice."

"Yeah. Well, it's good to see you. I should let you get back to the boys."

And he walked away from her, never looking back…

Chapter Twenty-Two

Dot lay in bed that night, replaying the brief encounter in her head. For forty-four days, she had been able to pretend she was okay with being alone. She had gone through every breakup stage: truly pissed off at Boone, then missing him, then reaching the point of acceptance around her new reality.

But seeing him at the rink? Shit! Shit, fuck, damn. That one glimpse of him that way, the look on his face when he hugged Finn, and her acceptance was gone. That man was the stuff dreams were made of, and she had blown her chance to be with him.

Except, he didn't accept her reality. That was the problem. Boone had been stubborn, wanting things his way, and that wasn't fair, or right. It was his fault they had broken up, and she was better off alone.

But was she better off alone? She let her mind wander back to an afternoon at his house when everything had been perfect between them. The boys had gone off hiking with friends, so she and Boone had spent the afternoon in bed. The sun was streaming through the window onto the bed that day, and they laid naked in the warm sunshine, talking, laughing, kissing like teenagers. The sex had been glorious. Then again, when wasn't sex with Boone glorious? He was so fucking sexy and handsome; his body could rival that of any Hollywood hunk, and yet, as a lover, he was all about her pleasure. Not to say he didn't enjoy himself too, but he clearly got off on turning her on.

It had started with a back rub that afternoon, but not just her back. He started at her toes and worked up to her scalp, just touching her, making her melt into the bed. Then, he turned her over and did the same on her front. He had gone out of his way to avoid being overtly sensual in his touch, but that made it even sexier. He asked her to tuck her hands behind her head, and he used his tongue to drive her crazy until she begged him to take her, right then, as hard as he could.

Just thinking about it made her so hot and wet. Damn him! If he wasn't so fucking stubborn, they could still be together. So, it would still be afternoons at his place and not spending the nights together? So what, they'd still be a couple. How could he say he loved her and then walk away like he did? Asshole. Sexy, irritating asshole.

Two days later, Boone came out of the men's locker room after practice, and found Finn sitting alone on the bench, his eyes shut. "Finn, you okay?"

Finn's eyes flew open. He was clearly shocked to see Boone. "Fine, Boone, just getting my skates on for practice."

Boone watched as Finn, with an enormous effort, shoved his feet into his already-laced skates. What was he doing? With a shake of his head, Boone grabbed his bag. "Night, Finn."

"Night, Boone."

It happened again two days later. Boone came out just in time to see Finn shoving his feet into the skates. "Finn, what's going on, buddy?"

The boy looked around. "Nothing, Boone."

Boone sat down on the bench next to him. "Hey, buddy, I'm going to go out on a limb here, but it seems to me you are having an issue with your skates. What's the problem?"

Finn's gaze dropped in embarrassment. "Please don't tell Mom or Dec. Please."

"Tell them what?" Boone felt his heart constrict in pain, seeing the stress on the little boy's face.

"That I can't lace my own skates." His eyes met Boone's. "Please."

"What do you mean, you can't lace them?"

Finn held up a leg to demonstrate his point. "Dec tied them for me a couple times, then told me I should be able to do it by myself now." His foot was jammed halfway into the skate, which was still tied. "Some guys have their dads help them," he shrugged, "but I can't ask Mom to come in here and help me, and I can't ask Dec again."

Boone felt a rush of love for the young boy, remembering firsthand how odd it felt to be without a dad. "Dude, I have a suggestion."

"Okay." Finn's eyes fixed on the skates again as he tried to cram his feet in them.

"I'll help you now, but after tonight, come around the corner into the men's locker room once you're dressed, and I'll do your skates there. No one has to know, deal?"

Finn's eyes lit up. "You mean it?"

"I do. That way, your mom won't know, neither will Dec, but you can have your skates fit the right way."

Finn threw himself into Boone's arms. "Thank you, Boone. Thank you!"

Boone kissed the top of the boy's head. "My pleasure, my friend."

Each night of practice, Boone helped Finn. And each time, Boone realized the little boy took a bigger chunk of his heart. Dammit, Dot. How could she not trust him in her life with her boys? He may lack personal experience as a father, but he could have learned. He could have taken a fucking class in parenting if needed. But no, she had to control everything. She wouldn't even give him a chance.

The local harvest festival was always a big weekend - the town picnic, a concert, an arts and crafts fair. Boone hadn't planned to go, but then PJ and Julia convinced him that going, and taking Julia's friend Katie, would help his mood.

The weather was perfect on the night of the concert, the ultimate Indian summer night. Standing by the bandstand with his tall, willowy date, Katie, Boone felt relaxed. It would be fun to drink a little, dance some, and laugh a lot with friends.

As Katie went on telling him about her job as a radiologist, Boone spotted Dot standing by the beer tent. She was staring at him, and she was visibly shocked.

Boone's eyes widened. Jesus, she was giving him the death glare. What the hell was she doing here, and why was she mad?

He followed her gaze. Katie. Shit, shit, shit. She was upset to see him here with a woman. But, seriously, she had been the one who wasn't willing to change, right?

Boone put a hand on his date's arm. "Katie, would you excuse me? I just want to run over and talk to someone about some hockey stuff."

Katie smiled. "Of course, Boone. I'll meet you over at the blanket with Julia and PJ."

"Perfect. Thanks."

The brunette walked away, and Boone made a beeline toward Dot. When he was nearly at her side, she turned her back on him. He leaned forward and whispered in her ear. "I think we know what happens when I see your perfect backside, cupcake. Is this an invitation?"

Dot whirled around. "How dare you!" she hissed.

He grinned. "How dare I what? Tell you I still want you? Yes, I do. Still love you? Hell, yes."

"You have the gall to say that when *you* were the one who dumped *me*?"

His eyes narrowed. "I do. And for the record, I didn't dump you, sweetheart. I told you it wasn't working for me the way we were. As I recall, I told you that when you were ready to try it a different way, to let me know. So now you're all pissed off because I'm here with someone else?"

"I am not."

Boone chuckled. "You're fucking green with jealousy." He studied her gaze for a moment, then nodded as a way of ending the discussion. "Fine, then have a great time. If you'll excuse me, my date is waiting."

Chapter Twenty-Three

The next morning, Dot got out of bed in a foul mood. Not only had she endured watching Boone with a gorgeous brunette who made a point of fawning over him, but Declan had been a little ass about going home, wanting to stay with his friends and walk around town. He had finally gotten in the car to go home, but not without sparking an embarrassing scene at the park.

Sometimes being a single parent really sucked. It would have been great to have Mike there to tell him to knock it off, and to shoulder some of the weight she felt as the sole disciplinarian. Every day, every hour, she was the only one taking care of all these things for her boys.

She rubbed her weary eyes as she looked in the bathroom mirror. She looked like shit, too. Tired, pale, and her hair could use a trim. Bracing her hands on the edges of the sink, she took a long look at herself. Who was she kidding? Yes, Declan was a puke the night before, but he was almost a teenager and had a lot of those moments. That wasn't what had her in a mood, and that wasn't why she hadn't slept most of the night.

It was Boone, plain and simple. Seeing him with another woman had hurt more than she expected. And she couldn't do a damn thing about it. His expectations weren't realistic, and she couldn't live with them. He needed to change, and he wasn't going to, that was clear. So, they were done. No matter that he'd said he loved her, he was still out with another woman last night. Was that really love? No, it wasn't. Hell, she'd gone *years* without a date after Mike died. That was true love. Boone's professed love was just a way to get under her skin and get what he wanted.

Her phone buzzed with a text. Georgiana, this early on a Saturday?

Hey, get up. I'll be there in ten minutes with donuts. Put on coffee.

What was this all about? Dot replied with a thumbs-up and hurried to get dressed.

Georgiana walked through the kitchen door with a large bakery box. "I got lots, so the boys can have some too."

The two women sat at the table, mugs of coffee in front of them. Georgiana snagged a vanilla cream donut from the box and then pointed. "Maple cream, for you."

"Thanks, Georgie." Dot took one and took a bite. "Love these."

"I know."

Dot put the donut down on her plate. "Cut to the chase, Georgie. Why are you here?"

Georgiana laughed. "Can't I just want to have donuts with my friend?"

"Hell, yes. But you have that look on your face, so just get to it."

"What the hell are you doing with Boone?"

Dot's tone became guarded. "What do you mean?"

"Dot, the man is head over heels in love with you. Besotted, in fact. And you seemed to like him a hell of a lot, if I do say so myself."

"I do."

"Then what the fuck is the problem?"

"It's simple, Georgie, it really is. He's not a parent, I am. I promised myself, and Mike's memory, that the boys would be my focus, and Boone doesn't like that."

"Bullshit. I can't believe you really think that's what's going on here."

Dot could feel anger bubbling up within her. "Georgie, with all due respect to our friendship, and the fact that I've worked for you, maybe this is none of your business."

"It is my business. One, because I love you. Two, because I love Boone. And three, because I love the boys and they deserve better."

That pushed Dot over the edge. She pushed her chair back, causing it to scrape across the kitchen floor. "Fuck you! How dare you say that."

"Jesus, Dot. I'm not saying you aren't a fabulous mom, because you are. You know that. What I am saying is: you can be fully committed to the boys and still have Boone in your life. He's not trying to be a mere sex partner. He's trying to be your life partner, dipshit."

"I don't understand."

"The trouble all started when he wanted you to go away with him for the weekend, right? The boys were going to stay with us. And you were mad that he made the plans without talking to you first?"

"Yes."

Georgiana raised her voice. "It was a goddamn romantic gesture, Dot. How could you have missed that? He was trying to provide the best of both worlds – to surprise you, and to also be good to the boys. He *wants* to be part of their lives, and not just as the cool guy who brings pizza."

"I know it was sweet, but he needs to understand that I am their parent, not him."

"And therein lies the problem."

"What?"

"Dot, if you want to make it work with Boone, or with anyone, you need to accept that man into your life fully. Let him make some decisions with the kids. Hear his opinion. Correct them when they act like little fucks in front of him. Don't keep anyone around just for the sake of eye candy."

Georgiana's wording amused Dot, and she chuckled. "Can we change the subject? He broke it off, and he was out with someone last night, as a matter of fact. He doesn't exactly seem broken hearted."

Georgiana rolled her eyes. "PJ and Julia invited Katie. He's been in a foul mood ever since the night you broke up. It's not like it was some hot date at the harvest festival – they were trying to cheer him up."

"Oh." Dot scooted her chair back in and resumed indulging in her donut. "I'll think about it, okay?"

"That's all I ask."

Chapter Twenty-Four

"You did… WHAT?" Boone cried.

Georgiana kept kneading the bread dough. "I went to Dot's today to talk to her."

"I can't fucking believe you, Gigi. I love you; I know you mean well, but you are so out of line." He stood up and grabbed his coat from the back of his chair. "I can't be here right now, I'm too pissed. Tell Jack to come over if he wants to run." He turned and stomped out of the kitchen, slamming the door on his way out of the house.

Boone sped down the mountain until he realized how fast he was going. Shit, he needed to get his head on straight. Georgiana had gone over to talk to Dot, so what? He had said what he needed to say to Dot, and she had clarified that it was her way or the highway, and he refused to walk on eggshells forever around those boys. And he damn well would not sneak around to have sex with the woman he loved because she didn't want the boys to know anything about it. If they were going to be together, there needed to be a plan for the future. Hell, he'd be happy to go to family counseling if it would help. But nooo, she'd been mad about the weekend, and she still had not said anything about what an ass Declan had been to him.

Wait a minute! Was he letting a twelve-year-old boy get to him? Him? A Navy fucking SEAL? He had faced the most dangerous of situations, and yet a kid was beating the shit out of him.

Pulling into his garage, Boone shook his head. It was time to go for a long run to see if he could clear his brain.

He returned home almost two hours later; his body exhausted but his mood greatly improved as he headed for the kitchen sink to get a glass of cold water. He drained the glass, then started for the stairs, needing a shower. As he passed the counter, he realized he had left his phone there before his run. He tapped the screen to see if he had missed anything.

There was a text from Dot.

Please call me.

Should he call? Of course he should. He hit speed dial and waited impatiently.

She answered on the third ring. "Hello?"

"Hi."

"Hi." There was a pause. "Thanks for calling."

"You're welcome."

"How are you?"

"Okay. You?"

"Okay." She sighed. "No, I'm not okay. I'm not fine, no matter how many times I tell myself, or goddamn Georgie, that I'm fine."

"Good to know."

"Why did you send Georgiana over here?"

"What?" He was completely taken aback.

Dot now sounded completely irritated. "If you wanted to talk to me, why didn't you just call? Why did you send her to talk to me?"

"I didn't, Dot. I promise you that. I almost killed her this afternoon when she told me what she'd done. If I had something to say to you, I would have said it."

Sitting on the edge of her bed, Dot couldn't decide if she was happy or sad to hear that. He didn't want to talk to her. He was moving on with his life, without her. Shit… "Oh," she said.

"Dot, what is this really about?"

It was time to act like an adult, no matter how much she wanted to climb under the protection of her duvet. "I think we should talk."

"Okay." He pulled out a stool and sat down. "Go ahead."

"I miss you."

His heart melted. "I miss you too."

"And I want to figure this out."

"Me too."

"But—"

"Could we instead use 'and' instead of 'but'?"

"And... I think we need to get some things straight before we even try."

"Like what?"

"Like, I need you to understand that the boys come first. I am their mom, and they will always be my priority."

"I never said they shouldn't be."

"You booked a getaway for us without talking to me and made plans for them!"

"Jesus, Dot. I was trying to be romantic. We had been together for months, and aside from our odd first night together at the hotel, we'd never shared a bed for an entire night. Forgive me for thinking that whisking you away for a weekend of relaxation, some pampering, sex whenever we wanted, and some alone time was a bad thing. You repeatedly said that if you were away, you only felt safe about leaving the boys with Georgiana, so I took care of that too."

"It wasn't the idea of the trip, Boone. It was that you did it without asking me. What if the boys had something going on and they couldn't do it because we were going away? You should have asked me first."

"First, we had shared our calendars with each other, so I knew what their schedule was. I know when Atticus gets wormed, for Christ's sake. Secondly, it would not be the end of the world if the boys didn't have everything exactly the way they want it once in a while. Somehow, they would have survived the torturous hell of hanging out with Georgie and Jack."

"Boone, I am their mother. I make decisions for them, not you. You are not their father."

Sadness hit him hard. "And that's the problem, Dot. I know I'm not their daddy, I get that. Mike was, and always will be. But I could be their dad now, or at least a dad-like figure for them. But you won't let me in. I'm okay as a plaything for you, and for them, but I'm not good enough to become an integral part of your lives. Mike has been gone for most of their lives, and I find it hard to believe that he would want you to be miserable. I find it even harder to believe that he would want the boys growing up without a steady male role model present. Maybe I'm wrong, but I don't think that's what any man would want in their absence."

"Don't you ever, *ever*, tell me what Mike would want. Go fuck yourself." And she hung up.

Chapter Twenty-five

Two weeks later, Boone stood in his driveway watching the dump truck deliver a load of firewood. Six cords to be moved and stacked so he could heat with wood this winter. Well, the good news was that he'd get plenty of exercise...

Boone got to work. The woodpile was well on its way by the time he realized he should really get something to drink, so he went inside for a bit.

Stepping back out into the cool fall air, he was surprised to see a bike leaning against the side of the garage. He thought he was seeing things when he rounded the corner of the house and found Declan stacking wood. "Dec?"

The boy glanced over as if nothing was odd about the situation. "Hey, Boone."

"What are you doing?"

"Dave Sampson said his dad was bringing you wood. I thought you'd like some help stacking it."

Well, this was a surprise. "That would be great, thanks."

The two stacked wood, and as they worked, Boone tried to hide a smile as Dec told him more than in their short time together than in the whole time he'd been with Dot. He talked about friends. Teachers. Hockey. His brother. It was like the floodgate had opened, and the words just poured out.

Finally, Boone stretched his back. "Okay, Dec. Let's call it a day. Want a ride home?"

"Nah, Boone. I've got my bike." The boy looked down at his feet. "I have some time tomorrow if you'd like more help."

"I'd love that." Boone paused. "Dec, does your mom know where you are?"

"Nah." He scuffed his toe in the dirt. "Mom lets me take bike rides during the day on weekends, as long as I take my phone with me."

"Okay."

"I'll see you tomorrow. About ten?"

"Great."

At exactly ten the next morning, Declan pedaled up Boone's driveway. Again, he talked and talked, and Boone listened, offering a few comments when he felt it was helpful. Suddenly, the boy stopped stacking and said, "Boone, how do you know when a girl likes you?"

Boone chuckled. "Well, a year ago, I would have been certain in my answer, but lately, I'm not sure I really know."

"You mean because of my mom."

Boone nodded. "Yeah. You know I like her a lot, right?"

"Uh-huh."

"And I thought she liked me."

"She does." Dec made a sound like a sigh. "It's always complicated with her."

Boone tried to hide his smile at the very astute assessment. "So, going back to the girl… What is she doing exactly?"

"Oh, you know," Declan began, "she smiles at me at lunch but won't sit at my table. I saved her a seat on the bus on Friday, and she didn't sit there, but then she sent me a text thanking me for saving the seat."

"Sounds like she likes you. Do you like her?"

"I do."

"Then keep trying."

When they were done for the day, Declan got on his bike. "Hey, Boone," he called. "Thanks for helping Finn with his skates."

Boone looked at him with interest. "You know about that, huh?"

The boy pushed one pedal with the toe of his sneaker. "I do. I'd do it for him, but the guys would give him shit if I did, they'd call him a baby. It would be worse if Mom helped, so no one but me and Finn know you do it. It helps him a lot. Thanks."

"My pleasure."

Almost every Saturday for the next month, Declan rode up the driveway to see if he could help

Boone with things. They finished stacking the wood, then they tore some old fencing down. They built a deck and a chicken coop together. And no matter what they did, they talked. Each time Declan left, Boone would sit and think about the conversation, wondering what continued to inspire the boy to see him.

The next day, a Sunday, Boone got up early for a long training run. He was running a full marathon the next month, and he needed to make sure he was ready.

The run was great. Coming up the hill toward his house, he took a quick look at his stopwatch and grinned. Good time on it too. Now for a shower, breakfast, and a day of lounging and watching football.

There was a car in his driveway. To be exact, Dot's car was in his driveway. That was either going to be a really good thing, or a really bad one.

By the time he neared the house, she was out of the car, and one look at her face told him this wasn't going to be pretty. He slowed to a walk. "Dot."

"What do you think you're doing?"

"Walking up my driveway after a run?" He couldn't help the sarcasm; he would be damned if he was going to let her chew him out on his own property.

"Don't be an idiot, you know what I mean."

He opened the door and motioned for her to follow him into the house. "You mean you want to know why Declan has been coming over here."

"I mean, I want to know why you invited him over without my knowledge."

"I didn't invite him. He showed up one day, then the next, then each Saturday. He comes and helps me out around here and talks to me. We seem to be enjoying each other's company, that's all."

"What do you mean he talks to you? What would he talk to you about?" She sounded floored as she realized her son was no longer sharing every little thing with her, exclusively.

"How about girls?"

"He's talked to you about girls?"

"Yes. And hockey. And Finn, and about a trillion other things. He talks, I listen. That's it, Dot. It's not a plot against you. The kid showed up, and I admit I like having the company. There is nothing sinister here. You want to be pissed off about it, go ahead. You want to ban him from coming here, be my guest. He'll fight you on it, but you're his *mother*, you make the decision." He pulled his sweatshirt off over his head. "Now, if you'll excuse me, I've had enough criticism. I'm taking a shower. You're welcome to stay as long as you want, but I'm done talking about this."

Dot drove home faster than she should have, scattering gravel as she flew into the driveway. Her mood was vile as she pounded up the steps, noticing the bike leaning against the porch railing. "Declan, get down here!"

Poor Finn came into the house, already able to hear the yelling from outside. Mother and son stood at odds in the kitchen, both clearly furious. Finn opened his mouth to say hello, but his brother cut him off. "And another thing, Mom. We aren't babies. We're growing up. We have rights too, and we like Boone. We want him around."

Before Dot could say anything, Finn turned to look at his mother. "It's true, Mom. We do," he whispered.

She shook her head. "I told you both, it's over with him. I need to focus on being your mom."

"So you can tell us how you don't have a life other than us because Dad died? So you can make us feel even more guilty? Really, Mom. Give it a rest, okay?"

Her son had never spoken to her this way and his words stung. "What do you mean?"

Finn jumped in, trying to smooth things over. "Mom, what Dec means is that we've always known you put us first. We know that. But sometimes, like when you told us you stopped dating Boone because you need to take care of us, it makes us feel bad." He nudged his brother. "Dec wasn't very nice to Boone, but even he's come around. We like him. We'd like to have him around."

Declan put his arm around his little brother. "Mom, we will always love Daddy. Always. But he's been gone a really long time, and we'd be okay with you having a husband, if it was Boone. We'd like a dad."

Dot stared at her boys for what seemed like hours. "I'm going to bed now," she said flatly. "There's frozen pizza you can microwave if you get hungry." And she walked away, climbed into bed, and cried herself to sleep.

Chapter Twenty-Six

Days passed, and neither Dot nor the boys spoke of their conversation. Life returned to normal, other than Declan being grounded for going to Boone's.

On the Wednesday following the discussion, Georgiana marched up Dot's steps and banged on the kitchen door. Dot looked startled. "Georgie, is everything okay?"

Georgiana hugged her friend. "All good, Dot. But the boys are worried about you, and so am I, so I'm here to tell you that you're doing something this weekend, and I don't care if you want to or not."

Dot gave a wan smile. "What am I doing?"

Georgiana grinned. "Good. We, you and I, are going to Montreal for Friday and Saturday, coming back Sunday morning. We are staying in a spa there. Massages. Pedicures. Manicures." She ruffled Dot's hair. "A haircut for you. Good food. Relaxation and laughter."

That sounded so good, but…

"Georgie, um…"

"The boys? They are going to keep Jack company. Jack and Shroom are going to do some work on the lake cabin, so the guys can help." She took Dot's hand. "C'mon, Dot. Admit it. You need a break, and frankly, the boys need one too. It's been a bit rough lately. Come with me for a girls' weekend."

Dot nodded. "I'd love to," she said, against her better judgement.

That Friday morning, Dot hugged the boys one last time. "Be good for Jack, okay?"

The boys both rolled their eyes. "Yes, Mom."

"And Jack, you know how to find us if anything, anything at all comes up."

Jack chuckled. "Yes, I promise."

Georgiana's car was barely around the corner when Jack grinned at Finn. "Okay, let's get this show on the road."

Declan pulled his phone from his pocket and dialed Boone. "They're gone."

"On our way."

When Boone and PJ got to Dot's house, Boone hugged Declan and Finn. "This is either going to work, or I have to move out of town."

Finn grinned. "It's going to work."

Boone spread the blueprint on the battered wooden table in the center of the old shed. He looked at the boys. "Your dad did a hell of a job planning this."

Dec nodded. "He did, and now you're going to build it. He'd like that." He paused. "I think you would have been friends, and I know he'd want Mom to have a real studio."

Jack and PJ reviewed the plans. "So, first we clean out and demolish, then we put it back together this way?"

"You got it."

PJ looked around. "Thank God it's already sheet rocked and insulated. Even has a heat source, cool." He buckled his tool belt. "We better move our asses; this is a lot to do in very little time."

The three men and two boys, with a Basset Hound for moral support, worked until late that night when Shroom and Mark came over with dinner. They all rose with the sun the next morning and did it all over again the next day. By late Saturday night, they had cleaned, primed, and painted the inside of the old building. They had installed a new front door, three new double-hung windows, and a huge window looking out over the fields and river. They had built the office space Mike had planned for the little loft, hung new lights, and then finally installed the flooring. The boys then hung pictures and a family photograph while furniture was moved in and the easel and art supplies were put in place.

Finally, Boone took the blueprints, with the faded note handwritten in the corner that read, *For Dot -- your Christmas gift this year is your studio. With all my love, Mike* and placed them in a custom frame he had built to hang just inside the door.

It was done. Boone hugged the two boys tightly. "No matter what, I'm really glad we did this for your mom."

Declan smiled proudly. "It rocks, Boone. Thanks for doing this with us."

Finn looked around happily. "Maybe Mom can stop working at the school and just paint, and maybe you guys can get married."

Boone found himself immediately choked up. "I sure hope so, buddy."

Chapter Twenty-Seven

Georgiana drove through the familiar streets. "Jack brought the boys back a little while ago, so you don't have to go back to the farm to get them."

"That's awesome." Dot looked down to admire her pretty pink nails one more time. "This really was such a good idea, Georgie. I feel better than I have in ages."

"Good." Georgiana signaled to turn onto Dot's road. "We all need pampering sometimes."

"I guess you're right." Dot grinned. "I am ready to see the guys, though."

"I bet. Jack shot me a text, letting us know they're there, and he said he would take care of lunch by picking up pizza."

"Sounds great."

Georgiana tried to hide her excitement as she pulled into Dot's driveway. Jack and the boys were sitting on the porch steps, Atticus asleep in the sun between the boys. "Wow, we have a welcoming committee."

Dot chuckled. "It seems we do."

As soon as the car was parked, Dot jumped out to hug Declan and Finn. "My boys! I've missed you!"

Declan's eyes grew wide. "Mom, you look awesome. I like your hair."

Finn nodded. "And your nails."

Dot's eyes narrowed as she looked at Jack. "Did you prompt them?"

"I didn't." He laughed. "They're just observant."

"Yeah, right." She hugged them again. "Thank you."

Finn couldn't stand it any longer. "Mom, come with us, we have something to show you."

This seemed out of the ordinary. "Okay, lead on."

Finn and Declan each took a hand and pulled her toward the back shed. As she saw the new door, her face grew pale. "What..."

Declan's voice was filled with pride. "We did it, Mom. We all helped. You have a real studio now so you can paint whenever you want. It's your space, just like Dad planned."

Dot whirled around to look at Jack and Georgiana. "You did this?"

"I just helped," said Jack. "The boys, and PJ, Shroom, and Mark helped. But this was really Boone's idea. Well, Mike and Boone." His voice cracked with emotion. "The two men who love you." He motioned toward the boys. "And the young men who love you, too. They all had a hand in this."

"Where is Boone?" She didn't see him anywhere.

Finn was wiggling in anticipation, and he couldn't help but nudge her. "Go see, Mom, go inside!"

Dot opened the door, feeling faint with the strength of the emotion. The studio was exactly what she had dreamed of. It was just as she and Mike had planned, right down to the colors of the walls and the light fixtures. It was beyond perfect.

Suddenly, she caught sight of the framed print, and walked over to it. Reading Mike's words again, seeing his handwriting, she felt his presence and a wave of peace wash over her. Jack was right. Mike and Boone had done this together.

Sensing someone, Dot turned. Boone was standing silently in the doorway, watching her reaction.

"Hi," she whispered.

"Hi." His face was unreadable.

"I don't know what to say, it's perfect."

"It's just as he planned it. Someone with your talent needs the space to work."

"Thank you." Tears welled up in her eyes. "I love this. And I love you."

"About damn time, Mom," Declan yelled joyfully.

Boone stepped into the room and the rest of the group cheered as Dot fell into his arms, crying and laughing.

Minutes later, Georgiana wiped her own tears. "Okay, Dec, Finn, let's go get some lunch for all of us, and let your mom and Boone have a few minutes."

Finn hesitated. "But…"

"Come on, Finn." Georgiana opened the door.

Finn shook his head. "But…" He looked at Boone imploringly.

Boone nodded at the boy. "Hold on a minute, Georgie. I asked the guys to stay for a moment." With a gentle hand on Dot's face, he smiled, then knelt in front of her. "Theodora Murphy, please do me the honor of marrying me?" He looked at the boys. "And forming a family together?"

Dot was so overcome with emotion, the most she could do was enthusiastically nod in agreement before she croaked, "God, yes."

Georgiana and Jack almost had to physically pull the boys from the studio for Boone and Dot to have a moment together. As soon as the boys closed the door, Boone pulled her into his arms, kissing her with every ounce of his love for her.

Finally, he stopped and stroked her face, gazing into her eyes. "Really, yes?"

"Absolutely, totally yes."

Just then, before Boone could respond, Dec and Finn came pounding up to the door, screaming her name. Dot jumped back to grab the doorknob, fear filling her. "What's wrong? What happened?"

It was Declan who finally could speak clearly enough through his excitement. "Mom, Mom, God, Finn, just tell her!"

"Tell me what?"

Finn's eyes were huge. "Mom, a guy just called. He wants you to call him right back. He's from the Art Institute."

Dot felt herself get dizzy when she heard his words, and she clutched onto Boone's arm for support. Finn continued, "Mom, he said it's good news."

Two hours later, Boone and Dot dropped the boys off at the rink for practice, and then drove over to his house. Inside the front door, he scooped Dot into his arms, and without breaking stride, carried her upstairs to the bedroom.

He laid her down on the comforter and moved to lay next to her. He grinned at her. "So, now that you're going to be a famous artist, will you still marry me?"

Dot's head was spinning with the excitement of this whirlwind day. She now had a beautiful studio, she was getting a full grant to do nothing but paint for an entire year, and most important of all and dearest to her heart, she would now finally, openly, forever love this amazing, stubborn, sweet, loyal, gorgeous man.

"I believe I will…" she said.

Epilogue

Fifteen years later, Boone stood in the doorway of the church vestry. Finn called to him. "Dad, Dec needs you."

Boone walked down the hall to the room where the groom was dressing. He popped his head through the open doorway. "You need me?"

Declan laughed. "Always, it just took me a while to not be an ass about it."

They had talked a lot over the years about those early days when Dot's oldest son had struggled with a new man in his life. Boone shrugged. "It took some time, but you made up for it." He walked over and helped Declan with his tie. "You look great."

"Dad, listen, I wanted to thank you."

"For what?"

"For loving us. For helping Mom live again. For giving us sisters. For making us a complete family again, and for never letting us forget about our father."

Boone pulled his son into his arms. "It has been my pleasure and a true honor. You guys have taught me more than anyone else in my life. I love you, son."

Finn walked into the room. "Five minutes."

"I'll go find your mom."

Dot was standing next to the front door, greeting guests. Her two daughters, Sophie, and Ruth, stood nearby, lovely in their bridesmaid dresses. This was Boone's family. His spunky, independent, gorgeous, insatiable wife, now a well-known artist who kept him on his toes every single day of his life. His sons and daughters.

He was indeed a lucky, lucky man.

Acknowledgments

There are so many people who support me on this writing journey, and I am so very grateful for the support. Thanks to Between the Lines Publishing for their belief in my books. Thanks to Cyn and Sutton for being the best editors ever.

I couldn't do this without my loud cheering squad. Thanks to Ben, Melissa, Marc, Pauline, Linnea, Shane, Kayla, Ryan, Sora, Amie, Rowan, and Shay for always encouraging me to continue to write.

Finally, thanks to Paul, who believes in me, cheers for me, holds my hand when I am down, and who shows strength, grace, hope, and love every single day.

Read on for a sample of
Tomorrow and Yesterday

Prologue

The air was so cold, it was hard for her to breathe. Who was she kidding? It could have been a balmy, sunny day, and she still would have felt the clogging tightness of her throat, air barely able to get through to her lungs. So, the biting late November air really didn't matter. The small shards of ice pelleting her face as the storm rolled in didn't matter either. Neither did the painful cold that was seeping through her jeans from sitting on the stone wall. Her voice trembled. "I don't even know if you'd still like chocolate or not." She looked at the sky, so dark and foreboding. "I wish we could have had the time to get to know each other as adults, Jake."

She sat on the seawall for a long time, looking out at the gray, raging ocean, her heart aching for what could have and should have been. With trembling gloved hands, she pulled the cupcake wrapper off the pastry, stuffing it in her pocket without caring if she dirtied her puffer coat. With tears running down her cheeks, she bit one half of the small pastry, swallowing the chocolate cake with vanilla frosting without really tasting it, or allowing herself any joy from the decadent confection. Then, with an angry motion, she threw the rest of the cupcake out into the ocean, seeing it bob on the waves for just a moment before it sank. "Happy birthday, Jakie. I love you and miss you."

Chapter One

Three months later, Delaney hugged her cousin one more time. "Go, that's the final call for your flight. Have a great trip, and love you."

He nudged her arm. "You could still come with us, you know. Hawaii would do you a world of good."

"Nah. You know me; I don't know what to do with myself when I'm not working. I'd make you all crazy."

"No, you wouldn't. C'mon, Del, go with us." He tried to think of a way to convince her, "Do something spontaneous for once! Just get a ticket and join us. I'll buy the mai-tais. Come with us!"

"Not this time. You go have fun." She shrugged. "Besides, I'll get home late tonight, and will get a couple hours sleep before work tomorrow."

"Seriously, you need to start taking a break once in a while."

She'd heard that so many times before. "Yeah, yeah, yeah."

Delaney sat at the gate for her flight—people watching and knitting—with one wireless earbud in, listening to a podcast about the use of mindfulness in modifying the behavior of young children. The space was cold, so she wrapped her scarf around her neck and up over the side of her head with the earbud.

Just then, an airline attendant came to the nearby desk. Delaney watched as a tall, dark-haired man strode up to the desk, clearly agitated. "Excuse me, I'm booked on a flight to San Francisco, but I just got a call about a family emergency, and I need to get back to Boston as quickly as possible. Can I get on this flight?"

The woman looked at her computer screen. "I'm sorry, sir. This flight is fully booked, and everyone has already been checked in, so I don't have any options."

His voice was sharper than he expected. "My brother and his wife just gave birth to their daughter, and she was born almost three months early, and is in intensive care. I need to get back home!"

Calmly, the woman said, "Sir, have a seat for a moment. Let me see if there is anything I can do."

"Thank you." James sat down at the end of the seat row nearest to the desk, willing himself to control his agitation.

While the attendant was on the phone and looking at her computer, James noticed a young woman sitting off to the side, knitting. Always on the lookout for interesting visuals, James noted the shades of gray with her. Black boots rested on a black carry-on. Charcoal gray leggings led to a medium-gray tunic sweater, a light gray scarf wrapped around her neck, and white-blonde ringlet curls were visible sticking out from under the scarf. The oddity of the picture was the painfully bright scarf she was knitting, creating the image of a rainbow cascading down over the grays and blacks. James wished he could take a few minutes to sketch the scene, but instead tried to commit it to his memory so he could sketch it later

Just then, the attendant cleared her throat, wanting his attention. James jumped up and strode over to the desk. He sounded hopeful. "Am I on the flight?"

"No, sir. I looked at all the options." Her affect didn't change. "I am truly sorry for your family situation, sir, but I can't do anything about it."

Desperation filled him. "Can't you do an 'all call' to see if someone would be willing to take a later flight?"

"I can only do that when the airline has oversold the flight. That's not the case here." She smiled calmly, used to unhappy passengers. "I'm sorry, sir, but I can't help you."

"There has to be a way!"

"There isn't." She stopped smiling. "I need to ask that you step away from the counter, please."

Delaney had watched the whole encounter with interest, feeling for his distress. As the man stepped back, she saw the look of pain and frustration on his face, and her soft heart clenched tightly. For a moment, she allowed herself to recognize how attractive he was, but stuffed that aside.

As he walked away from the desk, she saw him pull a cell phone from his pocket, and seconds later she heard him say, "Mom, I can't get there until tomorrow morning. The last flight to Boston is full."

Making a quick decision, Delaney stood up and walked to the desk. "Excuse me."

The attendant looked up from her screen. "Yes?"

"If I wanted to give that man my seat, could I?"

The woman's eyes widened. "Yes, I guess you could. I would need to void your ticket, then issue him one in its place."

Delaney slid her boarding pass over the counter. "Do it."

"You don't need to go to Boston?"

"I do. But I can wait until the morning flight. He can't."

"You understand that you'll still need to pay for your flight, so really, you'll be paying for two flights?"

"I know, it's fine." Delaney walked away from the desk, having been booked on the early morning flight to Boston. She could go to a hotel, or instead, she could just stay in the airport. As she contemplated the options, the attendant called her name. "Ms. Adams?"

Delaney turned back to look at the woman. "Yes?"

The woman motioned her over and lowered her voice. "You know I couldn't comp your flight for you, and I'm sorry about that because you were being really kind. But I can give you a pass to the airline's club, and I've reserved a room there for you so you can get a little sleep."

Delaney was touched, and her face showed it. "Thank you. I really appreciate it."

"My pleasure." She tipped her head slightly, smiling. "It's nice to see someone being kind to a stranger. Thanks for reminding me of the goodness of people."

Delaney gathered her bags as the attendant picked up the microphone. "This is United Airlines, paging the passenger who needs to get to Boston tonight for family reasons. Please report to gate 28B as soon as possible."

Sitting at the concourse bar several gates down, James heard the announcement, and leaving a hefty tip on the counter, he almost sprinted to the gate.

The attendant looked up at him and smiled. "I have a seat for you, if you'd still like it."

"Yes, please!" As he handed over his credit card, he looked at her quizzically. "How'd that happen?"

She gestured down the concourse. "See the woman with the black bag?"

James looked and saw the young woman he'd noticed before. "Her? She was sitting over there."

"Yes. I guess she heard you, so she came over and gave up her seat."

"Really? Why'd she do that?"

"She said she could wait to get to Boston, and that you couldn't."

"Wow."

Discover if Delaney can embrace her future by letting go of the past or will her painful past consume her.

Kris Francoeur, writer and educator, lives in Vermont with her family and a menagerie of interesting creatures. Kris also is a grieving mother, who has found joy and light again through the practices of conscious and deliberate gratitude, unconditional acceptance, and connection with nature. Kris writes with authority about grief and moving forward in our very busy and stressful world, as well as being an accomplished author of contemporary novels, and a successful ghostwriter. Kris loves to spend time with her family (including sons, daughter, and grandchildren), spending time in the garden and spinning the alpaca fiber for yarn for knitting.

www.ingramcontent.com/pod-product-compliance
Lightning Source LLC
Chambersburg PA
CBHW072011110526
44592CB00012B/1269